The Family Therapy Collections

James C. Hansen, Series Editor

Steve de Shazer and Ron Kral, Volume Editors

INDIRECT APPROACHES IN THERAPY

AN ASPEN PUBLICATION®

Aspen Publishers, Inc.
Rockville, Maryland
Royal Tunbridge Wells
1986

Library of Congress Cataloging in Publication Data

Indirect approaches in therapy.

(The Family therapy collections, ISSN: 0735-9152 ; 19)
"An Aspen publication."
Includes bibliographies and index.
1. Family psychotherapy. 2. Metaphors—Therapeutic use. 3. Symbolism (Psychology) I.
de Shazer, Steve. II. Kral, Ron. III. Series.
RC488.5.I49   1986   616.89'156   86-14034
ISBN: 0-89443-620-1

The Family Therapy Collections series is indexed in *Psychological Abstracts* and the PsycINFO database

Article reprints are available from University Microfilms International,
300 North Zeeb Road, Dept. A.R.S., Ann Arbor, MI 48106.

Editorial Services: Ruth Bloom

Library of Congress Catalog Card Number: 86-14034
ISBN: 0-89443-620-1

Printed in the United States of America

1 2 3 4 5

Table
of
Contents

Board of Editors

v

Series Preface

FAMILY THERAPY COLLEC-
TIONS is a quarterly publication in
which topics of current and specific interest to family therapists are presented. Each
volume serves as a source of information
for practicing therapists by translating theoretical and research conceptualizations
into practical applications. Authored by
practicing professionals, the articles in
each volume provide in-depth coverage
of a single aspect of family therapy.

This volume focuses on indirect methods in family therapy. Sometimes, communication is most powerful in its
indirect form. The indirectness allows
the clients a great deal of freedom in
responding to a therapist's intervention;
it permits the clients to use their own
creativity and resources in making
changes. The authors who contributed to
this volume present various concepts of
indirectness and numerous case exam-

ples that will encourage readers to consider and use indirect methods of
therapy.

Steve de Shazer and Ron Kral are co-
editors of this volume. Steve de Shazer is
the director of the Brief Family Therapy
Center in Milwaukee, Wisconsin. The
author of two books, *Patterns of Brief
Family Therapy* and *Keys to Solution in
Brief Therapy*, he is currently conducting
a research project to determine what
interview techniques are most effective
in therapy. Ron Kral is a school psychologist in the Elmbrook School District and
a research associate at the Brief Family
Therapy Center. He is the coordinator of
the Adoptive Families Program at the
center and is researching the impact of
adoption on family members.

James C. Hansen
Series Editor

Preface

W HEN WE BEGAN PUTTING together this collection of papers on indirect approaches to therapy, we decided to leave the definition of the indirect-direct distinction to the individual author's discretion. We expected two major themes: (1) Ericksonian indirect approaches and (2) Milanesque concepts of circularity and neutrality. From this starting point, we hoped to be able to develop a rigorous theoretical model that included both views of indirectness.

As Steve de Shazer began to write his article, however, he discovered that he no longer held an Ericksonian view and had to rethink the indirect-direct distinction. As it turned out, the other contributors also took more creative, idiosyncratic views. Consequently, our theoretical model began to look like a plate of spaghetti rather than a decision tree—and useful theories do not look that way. Thus, the reader has many options, somewhat like a diner who must pick from a menu. The contributors describe their main course in mouth-watering terms and tempt the reader to buy their offering.

Yvonne Dolan uses a pure Ericksonian definition; for her, being indirect means using metaphors, while being direct means telling clients what to do. Alex-ander Blount expands this concept of indirectness to include influencing the clients outside their awareness in order to surmount resistance and promote cooperation.

Bill O'Hanlon offers a different view, suggesting that the therapist use indirect approaches when treating complaints that do not involve the client in some deliberate action. Mary-Jane Ferrier equates indirectness with circularity and neutrality, an approach in which there is no intentional direct action by the therapist to influence the client in any particular direction. Michele Ritterman suggests that Erickson indirectly worked on the client's "outside" behavior while focusing on the "inside" and that Minuchin indirectly works on the client's "inside" while focusing on the "outside."

Steve de Shazer suggests that focusing on the development of solutions can be seen as an indirect way of resolving the client's complaints. Ron Kral uses the term *indirect* to describe therapy with adults only for a child-focused problem. Brian Cade examines the use of humour in therapy.

In the final offering, Kurt Ludewig disagrees with all the other contributors.

As we read the articles, one after the other, we were reminded of good murder mysteries in which new clues force readers to change their opinion about "who done it" in every chapter. Interestingly, none of the clues provided by the authors in this collection is a red herring, because they all prompt therapists to think about what they do and how they do it. Unlike vintage mysteries, this volume leaves the actual conclusion to the reader.

The sum effect, after reading all the contributions, resembles a Milanesque intervention. That is, the reader cannot feel pushed into accepting any one particular perspective, but instead is pushed and/or pulled into thinking more specifically about how to know when to do what. Any or all of the offerings may taste "just right." The choice is not "either" this one "or" that one, nor "if" this one "then" none of the others.

It is more like "both" this one "and" all the others.

One possible conclusion is that the indirect-direct distinction is useful only on a case-by-case basis and depends more on the therapist's construction of reality and the therapist-client interaction (constructing their reality through negotiation) than on some theory of indirect-direct therapeutic approaches. This may not be bad, since it indicates the importance of watching the client's reactions and doing something in response to those reactions. As Erickson might have said, once you have the snowball rolling down the hill, you cannot predict its path. But you better watch where it goes, so you can get out of the way!

Steve de Shazer
Ron Kral
September 1986

INDIRECT
APPROACHES
IN
THERAPY

1

Metaphors for Motivation and Intervention

Yvonne M. Dolan, MA
Consultant and Psychotherapist
and
Co-director, Milton Erickson
Institute of Colorado
Denver, Colorado

M ETAPHORS CONSTITUTE A valuable "shorthand" method of communication that enables patients in therapy to develop their own solutions to their problems. If derived from and carefully based on the clients' own experiences and perceptions, metaphorical techniques are likely to succeed when more traditional forms of therapy have failed.

Therapists may use metaphors and metaphorical techniques as teaching tools, vehicles for therapeutic communication, motivational devices, and instruments for therapeutic change. Because of their implicit indirectness, metaphors are a powerful tool for reaching even the most fearful or suspicious client. It is difficult to "resist" the help offered in a therapeutic message that is not overtly recognizable as such!

A metaphor represents or stands for that which it is not, much as a road map represents a state without actually being that state. After reading a road map, individuals may decide to change the direction in which they are traveling and later effectively carry out that decision by means of the knowledge obtained by looking at the map. A good metaphor provides clients with a quickly comprehensible map for current directions, awareness, and problem resolutions.

A therapeutic metaphor may not be comprehensible to the client, on a conscious level, but is understandable on an unconscious level. The metaphor elicits an unconscious search for an appropriate and adaptive solution to the problem. The precise meaning that a client attaches to a metaphor is derived from the client's own inner resources: memories, dreams, goals, fears, hopes, and unconscious learnings. Therefore, the resulting application fits the client's needs exactly.

CHARACTERISTICS OF EFFECTIVE METAPHORS

Metaphors are most likely to be effective if they reflect the key elements of the client's problem and the solution to the problem, but differ greatly in content from the actual problem (Dolan, 1985). When the story is vague in its direct applicability and yet "isomorphic" (de Shazer, 1982) to the client's situation, the client is impelled to search inside himself or herself to find an appropriate meaning.

The appeal of the metaphor may be increased if the therapist incorporates descriptive words derived from the client's idiosyncratic way of speaking. Bandler and Grinder (1975, 1979) suggested that people have preferred modes for taking in, storing, and later recalling information; these modes are based on the senses. An individual's preferred mode can be identified by the descriptive words that he or she uses. For example, a client who prefers to communicate in a primarily visual mode is likely to make statements such as "I see what you are saying," "That looks interesting," and "My view of the situation is. . . ." In order to communicate more effectively, the therapist can incorporate the client's favorite kinds of descriptive words into the metaphor. The metaphor's therapeutic effectiveness and appeal will be in direct proportion to the accuracy with which the therapist is able to identify and incorporate the client's perceptions and preferred patterns of communicating.

MOTIVATIONAL METAPHORS

With some clients, it is necessary to create a motivational metaphor in order to engage them in an unconscious search for a solution to the problem or even, in some cases, to define the problem. This is particularly true if a client has previously been in long-term therapy without positive results or, for any reason, has begun therapy too disheartened to work actively to solve the problem. Motivational metaphors can be used effectively with those "vague" clients who are obviously distressed, but are initially unwilling or unable to state what they want.

A motivating metaphor should contain a symbolic representation of the client's hopes and the client's fears of the consequences of failure to achieve the desired therapeutic change. Representing an idealized version of the solution to the problem, the client's hopes instill sufficient courage for the client to attempt and complete the therapeutic changes. The client's fears, while representing an exaggerated version of the problem, can provide the necessary initial therapeutic momentum.

Storytelling as a Motivational Technique

The therapist can create a motivational metaphor by telling the client a meaningful story that contains symbols for both hope and fear.

Carol was a 23-year-old client who had not worked at any job for more than 10 days during the past 18 months. She refused to live at home, but her concerned parents brought her to therapy after she had been arrested for petty theft. Recently, Carol had worn out her welcome with the last of a series of friends who had shared their living quarters and food with her. She owed money to virtually all her friends and relatives. She was in obvious distress, but was unclear about what she wanted from therapy.

Carol felt that most jobs reflected values that were contrary to her beliefs and that accepting such a job constituted "giving in." She felt a strong need to "rebel" against the values of a "hypocritical society." She had taken and then quickly abandoned a wide variety of jobs because they were not "meaningful" or were "beneath" her. She was continually hoping to find something better. Ironically, she told the therapist that her worst fear was to find herself on the street in cold weather with no food, no friends, and no money; this appeared to be the exact path that she was following. Carol stated that she had little desire to try something new; she felt too hopeless. At the same time, she realized that she could not continue living as she had been.

As an initial motivational device, the therapist told Carol two very brief stories that represented Carol's fear and hope:

> "Cleaning out the refrigerator to make room for new things is a good idea, but if a blizzard or other crisis happens during the lapse between getting rid of one set of contents and selecting another, a person, especially in the mountains of Colorado where you and I live, . . . could conceivably starve to death [fear]."
> "Even if the stuff you have to work with in the kitchen is essentially not what you want to spend time cooking, soup made from inferior stuff is still soup and can be nourishing until you are able to . . . comfortably procure something better [hope]."

Carol responded to the stories by saying that she needed to do something to take care of herself and wanted help in determining exactly what to do about her living situation and unemployment.

Enactment as a Motivational Technique

In some cases, the enactment of a metaphor can motivate a client more immediately than can a story. For example, Erickson resolved a client's sleep disorder by requiring him to polish the floor if he could not get to sleep at night. Quickly, the client began to sleep well (Haley, 1984)!

A young woman who, although slim and attractive, was obsessed with her weight became extremely anxious and fearful that she was gaining weight. A former anorectic, she tended to worry about her weight aloud, much to the annoyance of her husband. The couple sought therapy because they were about to leave on a cruise and they feared that the woman's obsession with her weight would ruin the trip for both of them. The husband's mother, a very unpleasant woman, had berated the young couple for spending the money on a luxurious trip rather than on more practical items. The couple, in fact, had saved their money for years in order to afford the long-anticipated cruise.

The wife had a very definite dislike for her mother-in-law and wanted little to do with her; she specifically mentioned that she hated to buy Christmas presents for her mother-in-law. Therefore, the therapist suggested that the wife buy a needlework project that was likely to please her mother-in-law for this year's Christmas present. Each time the wife began to worry about her weight, she was to get out the needlework project and work on it until she had finished worrying. The wife reluctantly agreed to do this because, as she stated, laughing, "I hate it, but it's probably the only thing that would work."

Three weeks later, the couple returned from the cruise. The wife had needed to work on the needlework project only once, at the beginning of the trip, and they had an amazingly worry-free time. On the last day of the trip, the husband had delighted his wife by throwing the needlework project overboard. Subsequently, the couple began to swim together every morning as a weight control device. There have been no further complaints.

In this sort of enactment, clients must act out their fears of the consequences of failure to achieve the desired therapeutic change. For this client, the ordeal of working on the needlepoint replaced the original problem of worrying about her weight, enabling her to focus on the solution. De Shazer cautioned that clients will agree to perform seemingly strange tasks only if the tasks are metaphorical representations of their own unique patterns "of cooperation" (de Shazer, 1980). As this patient volunteered the information regarding her dislike for her mother-in-law, it could be used to supply the motivational energy that the client needed to set herself free from the symptom of worrying.

Interspersal as a Motivational Technique

A therapist can also motivate a patient by interspersing the needed metaphorical messages within a story. In fact, a therapist may choose to tell a story simply to provide a background for interspersing indirect motivational messages (Erickson, 1966). The story can be about any topic that interests the client. The story then becomes a means for more important motivational communication.

A client complained that she had come to the end of her patience and that her life was bleak and meaningless. She felt unable to change, however, although she wanted "to do something." Her stated fear (problem) was that her impatience would just continue because her life would not improve; her hope was that something could be done (solution) although she did not know what. She was an avid gardener, but had little experience gardening in shady locations. The therapist interspersed motivational messages within the following casual talk about her own shady garden:

> "Walking out in my garden this afternoon, I noticed that the red flowers I had placed in the side planters were (*dropping voice conspiratoraly*) overflowing . . . that red IMPA-TIENS (*pronounced like the word, "IMPA-TIENCE"*) CAN REALLY HELP TO cover the bare spots. People told me that the back yard was too dark even for those IMPA-TIENS, BUT IMPATIENS CAN GROW in the very shady spots, making color and bring-

ing a garden to life. AND YOU CAN DO SOMETHING WONDERFUL WITH plants like IMPATIENS even in a terribly shady garden like mine. The only other plant growing in that side of the yard is a large healthy cluster of Silver Dollar plants, with their transparent coverings all ready to dry and EXPOSE THE BRIGHTER OTHER SIDE."

This story reflects and amplifies the client's growing impatience with her situation to create motivation. The impatience is then connected to the metaphorical solution of doing "something wonderful" with the impatience. The client subsequently came up with specific ideas of things she wanted to change in her life.

METAPHORS AS THERAPEUTIC INTERVENTIONS

Once the client has been motivated, other metaphorical techniques may be used as the primary therapeutic intervention. The distinction between motivational metaphors and therapeutic metaphors is not absolute, however. In some cases, the motivational metaphor alone enables the client to make the necessary therapeutic changes spontaneously; in other cases, the motivational metaphor simply opens the way for the client to respond to therapeutic metaphors.

Meaningful Stories

If a story is sufficiently representative of the client's problem and its symbolic solution, the client responds by unconsciously searching for a uniquely appropriate solution and subsequently makes the appropriate therapeutic changes (Dolan, 1985).

Despite her strongly verbalized need to "rebel" and "be free," Carol's enduring naivete and concern for the welfare of others made it difficult for her to succeed in her attempts to embrace the "street-wise" vocations of drug dealer and petty thief. She felt that more socially acceptable forms of employment were contrary to her own values, however. Faced with this seemingly hopeless dilemma, Carol felt that suicide was her only option.

Because direct attempts at therapy over the past 5 years had obviously failed to help Carol resolve the paradox of her simultaneous needs to express herself through rebellion and to provide herself with food and shelter, an indirect metaphorical approach was selected. It was necessary to develop a metaphor that included a representation of the problem, the need to rebel, and a representation of the solution, a way to rebel in a healthy and adaptive manner. The metaphor chosen had to be sufficiently interesting for Carol to listen to the full story. The therapist told Carol the following story:

"I don't think I've mentioned to you before that I'm a scuba diver. . . . A few years ago when I decided to learn to dive, I was in a bit of a hurry and didn't want to wait for a scheduled class, so I took private lessons from an old man. He told me, 'The sea is very unforgiving.' When you're going against the rules by being in an environment you aren't exactly suited for—I mean we don't have gills—there is a very real danger. If you make one too many mistakes or even make just one mistake at exactly the wrong time, you're dead. It's a dilemma, because it's so beautiful and free down there—you really want to be there and enjoy all that, and yet it can be very dangerous, resulting in death and/or permanent injury [problem: surviving while rebelling against the "rules"].

"Scuba diving is, however, despite the potential dangers of getting the "bends," drowning, or being eaten by a shark, an incredibly pleasurable activity. The pleasure of being really comfortable down there makes up for the potential dangers. Fortunately, it is possible to dive safely. All you really have to do is find out what the time boundaries are on the dive table and then dive as long as you like while following the charts and making sure that you have plenty of air to breathe during your return to the boat. Sometimes the water gets a little rough on the surface, but you can always find a calmer spot below the surface [unconscious] where you can think a little more clearly and find comfort and pleasure. Diving is one of the safe and healthy ways to do things that many people would consider breaking the rules of nature and simultaneously to explore the thresholds of being all you can be [solution: defying the "rules" in safe and healthy ways]."

A few days after hearing this story, Carol came to the therapist's office to show off a very radical haircut. She mentioned that she had just taken a part-time job in a used clothing store. She was dressed in a manner that would make a war refugee look, by comparison, extremely well dressed.

A week later, Carol telephoned the therapist to say that she had taken a second job, a full-time job at a fast food restaurant, and that her parents had reacted by letting her move back home temporarily and cautioning her "not to try to do everything at once." Her parents intuitively reacted in this wonderfully paradoxical manner. The result was that Carol decided to "rebel" further by taking a third job, part-time, and taking a shabby room at a rooming house.

During the next year, Carol worked diligently for approximately 60 hours each week, defying concerned parents and friends who were shocked at the rapid change in her method of rebellion. Then she complained to the therapist that she was tired of the counterculture "rule" that "you have to be poor to be cool." She decided to rebel against this rule by exchanging her three low-paying jobs for a better paying single job, beginning to dress in a tasteful and fashionable manner, and moving into a more comfortable apartment. There were no further conflicts with her parents, and she did not require further therapy for her original problem.

Apparently, the only intervention that Carol required was the metaphorical invitation to rebel in new, more adaptive and comfortable ways. The actual changes all came from Carol herself, once she had been given a new metaphorical "map" based on her need to rebel.

Enactment as a Metaphor for Change

A therapist may use metaphors as psychotherapeutic interventions by arranging for clients to enact in their homes metaphorical solutions derived from their own spontaneously stated metaphorical descriptions of their problems.

Susan, 16, lived with her father and stepmother. Her natural mother had deserted the family 5 years before. Occasionally, Susan received a card or a small gift from her mother, but there was never a return address. Susan was a model student and appeared to get along well with her father and stepmother. She denied feeling anything toward her mother, but she could give no explanation for two recent suicide attempts. She had begun to make a series of slash marks on her arms, "drawing" lines, with a razor blade on her skin whenever she felt upset. She was brought to therapy by her concerned father.

Attempts to get Susan to talk directly about what was bothering her were to no avail. She stated, "I just don't know why I feel so bad, there really isn't anything to talk about." She added that she would like to understand things so that she could feel "OK," but she "just found" herself "drawing lines" on her arms at times and did not know why.

Susan was told that it was important to draw lines when she felt upset, and she was asked to continue this practice. She was also asked to draw some lines on paper whenever she was upset, using whatever shapes and colors felt right, "so that you can learn even more about yourself." Because it constituted an enactment of her personal metaphor of drawing lines, the assignment was compatible with Susan's unique way of behaving and cooperating (de Shazer, 1980). Susan willingly began to draw in a notebook whenever she felt upset, although she continued to draw the slash lines on her arms at first. Within 2 weeks, however, she drew lines solely in the notebook. Her lines gradually evolved into evocative drawings of herself, her mother, and her feelings. After a month, she began to write words to accompany the pictures she drew. Two years later, she continues to keep her "line drawing notebook," expressing many feelings in it. There have been no further suicide attempts, arm slashing, or apparent depression.

A couple came to therapy and stated that, while they loved each other, they no longer felt the excitement they had felt when they were first married 3 years before. They stated that they had no sexual dysfunction problems, but they did not feel as "connected" to each other as they wanted. Two busy professionals with no children, they felt that they had become immersed in their careers at the expense of their marriage, often working long hours and spending their time alone together in discussions of their work. The husband said that, much to his despair, he was beginning to have "cold feet" about the marriage; the wife stated that she wanted to "get back in touch" with her good feelings for her husband. They both hoped that therapy could help them restore their original "feelings of warmth" toward one another.

The therapist gave the couple an assignment based on their own metaphorical description of the problem (i.e., the loss of "feelings of warmth," "cold feet"). They were to read a description of foot massage techniques from a good massage book. They were then to take a walk together after dinner. It was winter, and they were told to return home immediately as soon as one of them began to get cold. Once at home, they were to warm each other with foot rubs, hot drinks, and warm blankets, taking care not to talk about work. Subsequently, the couple reported that, although they had walked a little too long outdoors and become "a little chilled before the foot rub," they had proceeded to have a "thoroughly wonderful weekend" and were considering taking a massage class together. They did not know exactly what had changed, but they were happier and felt no need for further therapy sessions.

A rape victim came to therapy in tears. Despite a year of counseling after the rape, she was unable to enjoy sex with her husband. Anything that connoted sex elicited painful memories of her assault.

She was instructed to make a 2-hour tape recording of her favorite songs, including songs from her adolescence and young adulthood. She was then asked to listen to the tape while she and her husband watched an erotic film with the sound turned off.

Following completion of this assignment, the client was again able to enjoy sex. The songs provided a metaphor for the many positive experiences that she had enjoyed in her life and restored this pleasant context to her sexual relationship with her husband. A follow-up call a year later disclosed no further problems.

THERAPIST ENACTMENT AS METAPHORICAL INTERVENTIONS

In yet another technique for using metaphorical interventions, the therapist may enact in front of the client a metaphor that represents the current problem and its solution. When Cade saw a family that was hampered by difficulty in expressing feelings, for example, he arranged for his team to have a heated argument that could be overheard by the family (Cade, 1982). Following this episode, the family rapidly made therapeutic changes.

Erickson sometimes demonstrated to a client or a student that there was more than one way to look at things by literally heaving at the unsuspecting individual a metaphor in the form of an apparently heavy rock that was actually made of a lightweight and harmless material (Lankton & Lankton, 1983). Charlie Johnson (1983) sometimes conveys a similar message by showing clients Escher prints that seem different from various angles or by discussing a series of old maps on his door in which the erroneous information in the first maps was corrected on subsequent maps.

Some therapists who see a couple in conflict arrange to have, in the middle of the therapy session, a quick and very subtle argument representing each client's viewpoint. Approximately halfway through the argument, each therapist abruptly adopts the other's viewpoint, eventually ending the argument with a mild apologetic statement to the clients for "getting sidetracked." Generally, the clients become much more sympathetic to one another's views during the remainder of the session.

THE "MY FRIEND JOHN" TECHNIQUE

Erickson (1964) sometimes used metaphors about friends or other clients for therapeutic purposes, referring to this as the "my friend John" technique.

A victim of acquired immune deficiency syndrome (AIDS) came to therapy with the hope of finding relief from depression. The client's former lover had recently died; the client felt not only grief, but also a deep despair that he was probably wasting what little time remained for him to enjoy his own life. He requested help in separating from his pain so that he could "really live while . . . [he was] still able to live." The therapist told him the following story about another client:

"A woman client of mine decided to join an outward activity type of group to do some exploring and backpacking in the mountains. She thought that she was prepared for anything. She was in a group that was going to rappel approximately 100 feet down the sheer face of a mountain, holding onto a rope. Rappelling was the only way to get down from the cliff. Only the guide knew what was at the bottom, but the guide had given a very cryptic description. The distant view was somewhat obscured by an early morning mist. Apparently, the woman's partner was not strong enough to handle the physical and emotional challenge, or perhaps she simply lost her balance. Moments before the group was to begin the rappelling descent, the partner lost her balance and fell to her death. Everyone was deeply affected and horrified by the tragedy they had just witnessed, particularly the woman who now faced the dilemma of finding a way to complete her own journey as safely as possible while suffering the grief and horror of her friend's death. At that exact moment, the woman reported, a very odd thing began to happen. 'Certain parts of my body began to feel a tingling and then a peaceful sort of numbness, and then it was as if my mind began to function in a sort of detached way, too, as if in some inexplicable way I was being carried along effortlessly, as if supported by my partner's caring for me—it no longer felt like I had to make the journey totally on my own. . . . I

felt the support of the people around me, and the love my partner and I had shared as close friends. My legs and arms began to work seemingly on their own, and my hands gripped the rope securely and functioned competently despite a numbness. While the grief at the loss of my friend was overwhelming, I also noticed with amazement that I was somehow able to function with a courage I had not had before, despite a certain numbness that only left later when I felt comfortable.' "

At his next session, the client with AIDS described feelings of peace and a "sort of detachment" from his emotional and physical pain. Referring to his physical discomfort and the sadness regarding his lover's death, he said, "I know it's there and sometimes this week I let go and cried about it, and yet I've become so much more aware of the other things in my life this week . . . the friends I have now and the everyday things I want to do each day."

The accident of the friend and the dilemma that arose from the need to move down the mountain alone was chosen to represent the client's problem. The solution was represented by the unexpected resources of numbness (temporary dissociation from pain) and unanticipated courage derived from friendship. The client did not use the indirect suggestion for numbness to dissociate completely from the pain in a repressive way. Rather, he adjusted the pain to a more manageable level at which he could choose to "let go" and deal with it voluntarily instead of continuing to feel hopelessly overwhelmed and unable to function.

CONCLUSION

Solutions achieved by means of metaphorical techniques are likely to be highly appropriate because they are elicited from client's own unconscious resources. Because they are indirect, metaphorical techniques demand maturity on the part of the therapist, however.

Therapists are not likely to receive accolades or overly enthusiastic personal validations from clients who simply "find themselves" making appropriate therapeutic changes.

REFERENCES

Bandler, R., & Grinder, J. (1975). *Patterns of the hypnotic techniques of Milton H. Erickson, M.D., I.* Cupertino, CA: Meta Publications.

Bandler, R., & Grinder, J. (1979). *Frogs into princes.* Moab, UT: Real People Press.

Cade, B.W. (1982). Some uses of metaphor. *Australian Journal of Family Therapy, 3,* 135–140.

de Shazer, S. (1980). Brief family therapy: A metaphorical task. *Journal of Marital and Family Therapy, 4,* 471–476.

de Shazer, S. (1982). *Patterns of brief family therapy: An ecosystemic approach.* New York: Guilford Press.

Dolan, Y.M. (1985). *A path with a heart: Ericksonian utilization with resistant and chronic clients.* New York: Brunner/Mazel.

Erickson, M.H. (1964). The "surprise" and "my friend John" techniques of hypnosis: Minimal cues and natural field experimentation. *American Journal of Clinical Hypnosis, 6,* 293–307.

Erickson, M.H. (1966). The interspersal hypnotic technique for symptom correction and pain control. *American Journal of Clinical Hypnosis, 8,* 198–209.

Haley, J. (1984). *Ordeal therapy.* New York: Jossey-Bass.

Johnson, C. (June 1983). Personal communication.

Lankton, S.R., & Lankton, C.H. (1983). *The answer within: A clinical framework for Ericksonian hypnotherapy.* New York: Brunner/Mazel.

2

A Little Piece of Hell

Alexander Blount, EdD
Director of Clinical Services
Crossroads Community Growth Center,
    Inc.
Amherst, Massachusetts

INDIRECT THERAPY IS A CON-cept that begs definition in each instance of its use. It is the sort of notion that "all understand," but for which individuals may each provide a different definition. Indirect therapy inevitably creates the concept of direct therapy. Figure 1 depicts a slightly tongue-in-cheek distinction between direct and indirect therapy that implies two other categories. It is unlikely that this figure would be accepted universally in the field. Many practitioners of the direct therapies would insist that Quadrant 2 should be called "manipulation by the therapist." They would see the therapist's lack of openness about the process as dishonest.

On the opposite side stands Haley (1963), who rather elegantly equates the structure of the therapist-client relationship in psychoanalysis to the hypnotist-subject relationship. To Haley, the only difference was that analysts believe that clients' own internal processes guide their experience, while hypnotists are aware of their tactics to influence their subjects. In fact, Haley saw hypnotists as fundamentally more aligned with clients in that, through stories and other indirect approaches, they often allow clients to make changes without admitting the need for these changes.

There is no way to determine what a client actually perceives. Indirect therapy is an interaction in which it is helpful for the therapist to believe that he or she is influencing the client outside of the client's awareness, because this belief allows the therapist to act with clearer intentionality in the face of a sense that the patient would not cooperate with other approaches. It is an overarching stance on the part of the therapist in rela-

Figure 1 Direct vs. Indirect Therapy

	Therapist thinks client knows what is happening.	Therapist thinks client does not know what is happening.
Therapist thinks he or she knows what is happening.	**1.** Direct therapy	**2.** Indirect therapy
Therapist thinks he or she does not know what is happening.	**3.** Manipulation by client	**4.** Chaos: Call supervisor or systemic therapy

tion to the client rather than a particular set of techniques used in the therapy. Theories and techniques are, in fact, ways of allowing the therapist to connect clearly and powerfully with clients' experience and still maintain an intentionality outside the interaction patterns that the client effects when relating to other people.

Based as they are on the therapist's assumption that he or she knows what is going on in ways that the client does not, indirect therapy is often short-term. If the therapy continues for long periods of time, the therapist inevitably becomes part of a larger meaning system. This is problematical only if the therapist continues to operate within a theoretical framework that does not allow an analysis of this larger picture. If both client and therapist are assuming that the therapist is separate from and is somehow guiding the client's experience in the therapy and subsequent events suggest to both parties that this is not the case, therapy is on shaky ground, as in Quadrant 4. It was from the effort to

understand not just the family as a system but the family-plus-therapist as a system that systemic therapy arose (Selvini-Palazzoli, Boscolo, Cecchin, & Prata, 1978).

Systemic therapy is predicated on the belief that the therapist is part of the meaning system that develops in the room. The relationship of the therapist to the team demonstrates a pattern of relationship in which even the most influential person in the room is part of a much larger pattern of relating and understanding. In this context, the therapist can develop a redescription of the family relationships that creates a new reality for family, therapist, and team.

In the following case, the therapist used an approach that is probably best called "strategic." It was designed to be a short-term treatment. It could be called indirect therapy, both because some of the interventions were designed to be helpful in ways not expected by the clients and because they were designed to be helpful to people who were not seeking help.

Leanne called to ask for family therapy. She had recently had a meeting at school about her son, Bobby, age 12. Bobby had been in special classes for "slow" learners for most of his school career. Shortly before this meeting, however, Bobby had finally been given an extensive battery of tests. The results indicated that he had no identifiable learning difficulty. It seemed that he just did not do any work unless he was led through it step by step. His teachers had always assumed that this problem occurred because he had difficulty with his work, but his mother knew that this behavior pattern was not confined to school. She told the assembled staff at school that Bobby never did anything at home either unless he was continuously pushed to do it. The school staff suggested family therapy. Even though the school year was almost over, it was felt that some change was necessary over the summer if Bobby was not to fall hopelessly behind in the next year.

On the telephone, Leanne said that she would be glad to bring her daughter Terri, age 9, and even the baby, age 4, but she was very doubtful that her husband would come. She explained that he was already in therapy at the local Veterans Administration (VA) clinic for post-traumatic stress syndrome and was not willing to undergo any other therapy. The therapist replied that it had not yet been decided whether therapy would be offered to any of her family, that the decision could be made only after a few assessment sessions, and that Robert, her husband, would be

expected to come because he inevitably had special insights into Bobby's situation. It was left to the parents' judgment whether to bring the 4-year-old. An appointment time was arranged.

At the first session, Leanne sat on the couch next to Bobby with Terri on the end. Robert sat in a separate chair. He was extremely tense, but tried hard to be engaging. It seemed important to him that the therapist like him. Leanne described the happenings at school, and Robert related each to his "PTS." He said that Bobby was worried about him because of his post-traumatic stress and that this worry kept Bobby from concentrating in school. At home, Bobby did not do anything, according to his father, because he was depressed. He was depressed because he felt responsible for all the family's troubles, when, in fact, all the family's troubles were due to his (Robert's) PTS. Robert could not tolerate sternness, which he equated with violence, and was never able to discipline Bobby. While he talked constantly about his PTS, Robert had never said anything about his experience in Viet Nam to his wife. He believed that any sharing of the experience by him would allow the contamination it represented to be loose in his family.

Robert had been hospitalized at the local VA hospital for 2 weeks approximately 18 months earlier. His hospitalization followed a period in which he drank heavily, stayed out late, missed some time at his job, and was unresponsive to his wife's pleas that he come home and stop drinking. Since his time in the hospital, he rarely failed to comply with any of his wife's wishes, except for those times when his PTS made him "too nervous" to do what she asked of him. He remained chronically controlling and chronically alienated in the family.

Bobby and Terri agreed that their parents worried more about Bobby and fought more about Terri. She was openly resistant to her father. When he demanded that Leanne discipline Terri, Leanne defended her. Leanne did not see why she should help Robert with Terri when he did not help her with Bobby.

At the end of the first session, it seemed important to refocus on Bobby. If Robert were defined as the problem, it was unlikely that therapy would be possible. He had made it clear that he was not interested in any therapy for himself outside his ongoing work at the VA clinic. The therapist told the family that they were all people who were willing to take the blame for family problems in order to help other family members. This was part of their remarkable commitment to each other. The therapist added that, in trying to be true to their original request, he was willing to work only on Bobby's school problem and that they had convinced him of the connection between this problem and Bobby's lack of "self-esteem" (a favorite word of his father's).

As part of an assessment of Bobby's self-esteem problem, the therapist asked them to try an experiment. Leanne was to keep a log of the days on which Bobby made his bed. (She had said earlier that this would

be the first step in his beginning to do his chores at home.) Robert was to keep a log in which he rated Bobby's self-esteem each day. They were not to share these records with each other. Nothing else in the family's routines was to be changed. The assignment was designed to give the family the experience of having the parents cooperate in helping Bobby. This would happen no matter what the parents did, because no one else in the family would know if one or both failed to do their part. The assignment was given in a way intended to maintain the "assessment" definition of the therapist's relationship to the family. There was as yet no definition for the therapy in which Robert would be willing to participate.

At the beginning of the second session 2 weeks later, Leanne sat in the separate chair. She reported that Bobby had made his bed more frequently. Robert said that he did not think making his bed was the real issue for Bobby. There was an awkward silence. Then Terri warned the therapist that her mom and dad might start fighting again. She said that, just before the session, her mom was very angry and was throwing things around the house. It seemed that the parents were on the verge of a powerful scene. If that happened, the definition of Bobby as the problem and with it the access to Robert in sessions might be lost. On the other hand, glossing over such an important event seemed likely to disenfranchise the therapy as a setting for change.

The therapist chose to discuss the parents' fight, but used the children as primary informants. The approach was one of helping the children to understand that mothers and fathers have such scenes when they are really working on behalf of their children. Every once in a while, the therapist asked one of the parents for a detail. Complimenting the expressiveness and flair of the parents, the therapist began to build a team with the parents to help the children become more comfortable with what they had seen. The focus remained on the children, especially Bobby. As everyone had agreed that Bobby tended to blame himself for family problems, it was not hard to make the case that learning about his parents' fight would help Bobby.

It appeared that, although Robert had not changed his outward behavior toward the children, the possibility that he was covertly participating in their care had slightly modified his status as the wounded parent. This allowed Leanne to experience and express her intense resentment at his past failure to help her in guiding the children. In the same way, Bobby's making his bed showed his mother that he was capable of helping out around the house and made her furious that he had not done so before.

The parents listened carefully to everything that the therapist said to the children. They seemed calmer after learning that the fight was not taken as a sign that their situation was deteriorating. The focus stayed on Bobby as the couple's viewpoints were discussed. At the end of the session, the children were sent out and a therapy contract offered. The therapist said that therapy would be designed to help Bobby and would involve telling stories to Bobby in the context of family sessions. It was explained that these stories had been found to be helpful to children in his situation, but that no one knew exactly why they helped. The chances for the therapy were detailed: 60% chance that it would at least be worth the money, 10% chance that it would make things worse, and 30% chance that it would be no help. The therapist said that everyone should be there to keep Bobby from feeling singled out as the problem. Robert thought this was very important.

As Robert and Leanne left, the therapist congratulated them on their dedication to each other. They could make things easier on themselves, but they did not for the other's sake. Leanne could stop being frustrated at Robert's failure to help her, but that would remove the push for him to get over PTS; Robert could help Leanne a little more, but that might keep her from accepting PTS as an inevitable part of their lives. Because this was said after the session was "over," it did not refocus the therapy on the couple.

The third session was held 1 month after the second. Everyone seemed more comfortable. The parents appeared significantly less alienated from each other. They sat together on the couch with Bobby, and Terri took the chair. Again, the children were the main informants, but this time the therapist never turned to the parents for information. The children said that Robert had moved out shortly after the last session. He was gone for a week. Leanne had done well in his absence. At the end of the week, he had returned on a trial basis. Since that time, he had begun to discipline them as much as their mother did. He had grounded both of them for various offenses. Now they had to do much more work on their rooms, and he had even said that he was going to check homework when school started. Both children said that it was not fair to have two parents who grounded them. The therapist replied that they certainly had more to cope with and that he was reminded of a story.

The story was designed to help Robert. The therapist hoped that the story would offer him options in understanding his Viet Nam experience in relation to his family. During the telling of the story, the therapist looked at Bobby, occasionally glancing at Terri. Both were very attentive.

"There was a man who had always wondered what Hell was like. He thought about it a lot. One day the Devil appeared and offered him a chance to visit Hell and see what it was like for himself. He was scared to go, because he thought the Devil would keep him there. He asked the Devil to promise that, no matter what happened, he would be allowed to come home that day. The Devil agreed. Suddenly, the man found himself on a boat. The boat was on a river moving through a steaming jungle. Gradually, the river was going faster and faster. It seemed to be rushing down into the earth, as if into the mouth of a volcano. The air was getting hotter and hotter. Suddenly, the boat slowed. It seemed to be on an underground lake. The man strained to see, but the heat was so intense that everything was a blur. He thought he could make out peo-

ple on the shore of the lake, but he could not tell what they were doing. The heat was so strong that it seemed to burn up any sound. Then he saw the Devil coming toward him across the lake, standing in a boat. Two little devils were poling the boat. He was holding something. It was a little pot, like a coffee pot, but it had two handles, one on each side. As he reached where the man was, the Devil held the pot out to him. "In this is a piece of Hell," he said. "It is for you to take home." The man reached out to take the pot. The handles were so hot that they seared his hands. He tried to pull his hands back, but the little devils grabbed his hands and shackled them to the handles.

"Suddenly, the man was home, still shackled to the burning pot. It wasn't long before his family found him. He shouted to them that they must stay away, that the pot was too hot, and that he didn't want anyone else to get burned. His family wanted to work to remove his shackles, but he wouldn't let them. For a long time he suffered, waiting for the pot to cool, and his family watched him suffer. Finally, when he was asleep, his family crept close to him. They saw that the pot had a little door on the side that the man could not see. One reached out with a stick and pried the door open. The room filled with heat and light. The family pulled back, and the man woke up. He tried to close the door, but he could not. In that bright room, so hot from the inside of the pot, the man could feel the pot begin to cool. Before long, he was holding it without pain, and soon after that, his family was able to get close enough to help him break the shackles and put the pot down."

When the story was over, the therapist ended the session. As the family members collected their things and began to walk out, Robert clapped the therapist on the back. He said that he was glad that therapy was really getting started, but wanted to be sure that the therapy was for Bobby. The therapist told him that Bobby's problems were behind everything. He seemed happy with the session and with the therapist's answer.

The family, minus Leanne, came to the fourth and last session 6 weeks later. Leanne had been sick for the last week and was in the hospital, although she was expected to be released the next day. The therapist looked for any indication that the illness was stress-related, perhaps somehow expressing Leanne's position now that Robert was more active. The children's response did not help the therapist determine the answer to this question. Robert said that Bobby had been hard to motivate because he was worried about his mother, but he (Robert) understood. Besides, in his bad times now Bobby was so much better than he had been in his good times before.

As the session progressed, the therapist began a story that was similar in structure to the first—a person with a painful secret ultimately shares it with those close to him and is able to solve his problems. When the story was over, the therapist talked with Robert alone briefly. The therapist asked if he saw any pattern in the stories, and he said that he did. In addition, the therapist asked Robert if he would be willing to tell such stories to Bobby twice a week. Robert was anxious to try. Then the therapist suggested that, with school starting in a few weeks, they make no appointment, see how the year started for Bobby and call if things did not go well. They never called.

One year after the last session, Robert and Leanne were sent a standard follow-up questionnaire.

Leanne filled out the form. She said that Bobby's problem was "much better" and that there had been no other major incidents or changes in the family. When asked if they had had any further therapy, she said that she had joined Al-Anon. She also commented that the therapy seemed to end abruptly.

It seems reasonable to call this case a success in terms of the original problem. The indirect approach allowed therapy that might otherwise have been impossible. It allowed issues to be discussed without redefining the therapy in ways that would have jeopardized it. In the end, Bobby's school problem was "much better." He had received no further treatment. It is likely that the school staff would have insisted on additional therapy if Bobby had not been doing noticeably better.

In terms of the overall functioning of other family members, the results are slightly more equivocal. Why did Leanne need to join Al-Anon? If Robert had been drinking all along, this might be a good sign. She said there were no new problems, but there is still room for concern. It certainly would have been better to give the family a summary of their therapeutic status when it became clear that they were not going to call back. That would have corrected any problems in communication engendered by Leanne's inability to attend the last session.

The gains that were made as a result of the therapeutic process were due to the philosophy behind indirect therapy. This model allowed the therapist to go forward comfortably when it was said that Robert would not participate, to address a marital problem that could not be discussed without undermining the therapeutic contract, and to approach Robert's "PTS" without violating his need to be true to his other therapist. Perhaps the story taught Robert something fundamental. More important, however, it made the therapist excited and optimistic about the case. He was able to act with intentionality and with clear expectation of success in a situation (as it was originally defined) in which success was impossible.

REFERENCES

Haley, J. (1963). *Strategies of psychotherapy*. New York: Grune & Stratton.

Selvini-Palazzoli, M., Boscolo, L., Cecchin, G., & Prata, G. (1978). *Paradox and counter paradox*. New York: Aronson.

SUGGESTED READINGS

Bateson, G. (1972). *Steps to an ecology of mind*. New York: Ballantine.

Blount, A. (1985). Toward a "systematically" organized mental health center. In D. Campbell & R. Draper (Eds.), *Applications of systemic therapy*. New York: Grune & Stratton.

_____ (1982). The strategic use of the affective experience of the therapist. *Journal of strategic and systemic therapies, 1*(3), 24–30.

Hoffman, L. (1981). *Foundations of family therapy: A conceptual framework for systems change*. New York: Basic.

Selvini-Palazzoli, M., Boscolo, L., Cecchin, G., & Prata, G. (1980). Hypothesizing-circularity-neutrality: Three guidelines for the conductor of the session. *Family Process, 19*, 3–12.

Weakland, J., Fisch, R., Watzlawick, P., & Bodin, A. (1974). Brief therapy: Focused problem resolution. *Family Process, 13*, 141–168.

Watzlawick, P., Weakland, J., & Fisch, R. (1974). *Change: Principles of problem formation and resolution*. New York: Norton.

3

The Use of Metaphor for Treating Somatic Complaints in Psychotherapy

Bill O'Hanlon, MS
The Hudson Center
Omaha, Nebraska

ACTION COMPLAINTS VS. EXPERIENCE COMPLAINTS

ONE APPROACH THAT THIS author uses in deciding whether hypnosis and metaphorical techniques are appropriate in therapy for a particular client is to determine whether the client's complaint is an action complaint or an experience complaint. Action complaints involve the behavior of the person who is seeking the therapist's help, and experience complaints involve affective or somatic difficulties. For action complaints, the author typically uses a directive, action-oriented approach (O'Hanlon, 1982; O'Hanlon & Wilk, 1986) termed *pattern intervention*. For experience complaints, this author typically uses an indirect approach, usually involving hypnotic and metaphorical methods, that does not require deliberate action by the client. Of course, this is only a general guideline, one that can be ignored when the therapist deems it appropriate.

Actions may be treated as voluntary and experience as involuntary. If a client reports that he is having arguments with his wife, for example, the client may be able to alter some actions deliberately in order to affect the arguments. That is an action complaint, and this therapist would typically try to solve it by helping the client to change his actions. If, however, a client reports that she gets a rash every time she goes to the supermarket, it is unlikely that she could do anything different (aside from avoiding the supermarket) to stop the rash. Therefore, this therapist would typically use interventions that do not require the client to change her actions deliberately (i.e., indirect interventions).

WHAT'S A META FOR?

Transfer of Know-How across Contexts by Indirect Means

The etymological meaning of the word *metaphor* suggests the function of a metaphor in therapy. The word is derived from the Greek roots *pherein*, which means to carry, and *meta*, which means over or beyond. A metaphor carries knowledge across contexts, beyond its initial context into a new one. The purpose of a metaphor in therapy, thus, is to transfer skills (more colloquially, know-how) from the context in which the person developed or uses it to the context in which it would solve the problem that brings the person to therapy.

As a literary device, a metaphor may be a simile (i.e., something spoken of as "like" something else); for example, "Your smile is like the *summer sun*." In addition, a metaphor may be an analogy (i.e., something spoken of as if it were something else); for example, "We seem to have reached a *dead end* in this discussion." Such phrases are so commonly used that they are not always recognized as metaphors. These devices are used to *cast a different light* (another metaphor) on the subject. Everyone has experienced a summer sun, so it is easy to imagine that a smile likened to it would be bright. Everyone has seen the dead end of a road, so it is easy to understand the analogy when it is used to characterize a discussion. Metaphors make it possible to use understandings or experiences that have already been acquired to understand and make sense of new experiences.

Physiological and Experiential Competence

Therapists who use metaphors and other indirect approaches assume that people already have the know-how to solve the problems that have been troubling them. Clients have developed and mastered these abilities only in certain contexts, however, and are not currently using this know-how in the contexts of the problem.

To solve somatic problems, clients can use the physiological and experiential knowledge or competence that they already have. Almost everyone has blushed at some time, for example, and this ability to alter blood flow can be extremely useful in eliminating or ameliorating a headache. The biofeedback technique of warming the hands to eliminate a headache is well-known. Most people have felt their muscles relax automatically when they eased into a hot bath and the warmth of the water surrounded their bodies. This is not usually considered an ability, but it can be useful in helping people with chronic muscle tension or spastic colitis. The body can relax muscles, alter blood flow and body temperature, fight and eliminate infections, and alter body chemistry, among other things. This physiological know-how is not always used where and when needed, however.

In addition to physiological competence, everyone has a variety of experiential abilities and know-how. These abilities involve primarily the interpretation of perceptions and the direction or focus of attention. For example, people who are absorbed in a good book may not hear when someone calls their name; that ability, called negative hallucination in hypnosis circles, is a good method of pain control. People who have lived in colder climates may have found themselves unable to tell whether the water is hot or cold when they put their cold hands under running water. This ambiguity of sensations is another useful resource for pain control.

CASE EXAMPLES

Treatment of a Husband with Phantom Limb Pain and His Wife with Tinnitus

A man sought Erickson's help for persistent pain in a leg that had been amputated. His wife also reported that she had tinnitus (i.e., ringing in the ears). Erickson began the session by telling the couple that, when he was traveling around during his college days, he slept one night in a boiler factory. During the night as he slept, he learned to blot out the sounds in the factory and, by morning, he could hear the workers conversing in a normal conversational tone. The workers were surprised by this, as it had taken them much longer to master this skill; Erickson said he knew how quickly the body could learn. Next, Erickson told the couple that, the night before, he had seen a TV special about nomadic tribesmen in Iran who wore several layers of clothing in the hot desert sun, but seemed very comfortable. During the session, he told a number of stories that illustrated the ability of various people to become so habituated to any constant stimulus that they can "tune it out." This is the know-how that could solve both the couple's problems (Erickson & Rossi, 1979).

Treatment of a Boy with Enuresis

In his treatment of a boy who wet his bed, Erickson used analogies to help the boy solve his bedwetting problem by means of abilities developed in other contexts. The boy played baseball, and Erickson launched into a long dissertation about the fine muscle control that was necessary to be a good baseball player. The outfielder must open his glove just at the right time and clamp down just at the right time. In order to throw the ball to the infield, the player must release the ball just at the right time; if the release is too early or too late, the ball does not go where the player wants it to go. Next, Erickson told the boy about his digestive tract; he explained that the food goes into a chamber where muscles at either end close down for the proper amount of time, relaxing and releasing the food when it is time to move it to another chamber. He talked to the boy about the focusing of the eye, involving the eye muscles, that is entailed in archery. These analogies had a common theme of automatic control of muscles, just what the boy needed to use to stop wetting his bed (Haley, 1973).

Treatment of a Woman with Warts

A woman sought therapy for persistent warts, which were located mainly on her hands. She had been to a dermatologist regularly for 18 months to have the warts removed by freezing. This approach had painful aftereffects, however, and the warts kept returning. She sought hypnosis, because she had heard that hypnosis could cure warts. After helping her into a trance, the therapist told her how irrigation ditches were used in Arizona to water the plants and how pipes were used to irrigate each row of crops. When the pipe was removed from a row, the hot desert sun would wilt the weeds, which were more fragile than the crops. Similarly, the therapist told her, her body knew how to regulate blood flow so that nutrients would be withdrawn from the warts, but her skin would be kept alive. The therapist gave her the task assignment of soaking her feet first in the hottest water she could tolerate for 15 minutes, then in the coldest water she could tolerate for another 15 minutes. Several other analogies were offered, such as how she blushed automatically, and how the blood went to her digestive area after she ate a meal. All these were to transfer her ability to alter her blood flow and, thus, eliminate the warts. Three sessions of this type of treatment were sufficient to clear up the warts. Regular follow-up of several years has indicated no recurrence.

Treatment of a Woman with Asthma

A woman was referred for therapy because of a "pregnancy phobia." During the assessment process, the therapist discovered that the woman had been pregnant once before and had almost died on several occasions during and after the pregnancy, owing to asthma and bron-

chitis. Her period was late that month, and she had become quite anxious; her anxiety was accompanied by difficulty in breathing. Telling her that he did not think she had a phobia at all, but a quite realistic fear, the therapist suggested that hypnosis might help her to "breathe easier." After inducing a trance, the therapist reminded the woman that she had probably experienced automatic muscle relaxation when in a hot bathtub. The therapist suggested a complete body dissociation and hand levitation, both of which involved automatic muscle control. Reminding her of a well-known TV commercial that showed the opening of "blocked bronchial tubes" and the relaxation of muscles around the bronchi, the therapist told her that her body had previously ended bronchitis and asthma attacks and, thus, knew how to relax her bronchial muscles. The client had several sessions and experienced significant relief. She had learned she was not pregnant soon after treatment started; after she experienced such improvement through treatment, however, she and her husband decided to have the other child that they had wanted. She came in regularly through her pregnancy (for "booster shots") and experienced none of the breathing difficulties that she had experienced in the first pregnancy.

Treatment of a Man with Cluster Headaches

The man who was seeking therapy for cluster headaches described them by saying that they are like migraines, except that they come in groups. A phase might last days, weeks, or months, with one severe headache following another. The victim never knew how long they would last. "They call 'em .45-caliber headaches," he said with a finger to his temple, "'cause when you have one you want to blow your head off." After inducing a trance (although the client was never convinced that he was indeed in a trance throughout the two sessions), the therapist used several analogies:

- He may have been so absorbed in a movie or a good book that he did not notice that he had to urinate (to suggest dissociation or negative hallucination).
- He may have experienced that peculiar ambiguity of sensations that makes it impossible to determine if the water is hot or cold when cold hands are put under running water (to suggest reinterpretation of the sensations).
- He probably had felt the peculiar sensation (or rather lack of sensation) that arises when his leg falls asleep (to suggest anesthesia).
- He may have waited for some anticipated event, such as the end of the school day or the arrival of a check in the mail, and noted that time seemed to slow down and stretch out subjectively. The therapist suggested that the patient slow down and stretch out when he felt good or comfortable.

The therapist told the client that he had all these abilities and more, but there was no way to determine which one or ones would be most useful, how quickly he could find relief, or whether that relief would be total or only partial. (These last suggestions are examples of another type of indirect intervention, in which presupposition or implication is used to create an expectation of success.) Follow-up indicated that the client had experienced the beginnings of a headache the day after the second session, but they had quickly dissipated. No further recurrence of the headaches was reported. A year later, this client sent the therapist a co-worker who also suffered from cluster headaches.

GENERATION OF METAPHORS FOR TREATMENT

The first step in generating metaphors for the treatment of somatic problems is to think of the physiological or psychological solutions that are possible. There is no search for psychological or interpersonal causes or functions, only a search for the physiological change or shift in focus of attention that would solve the problem and help the person feel better. It may be that the client can be distracted from feelings of discomfort (a shift in focus of attention). It may be that the client's body can alter blood flow to relieve the pressure in the head so that the client no longer has a headache (a physiological change). It may be that the client can "develop callouses" for pain so that he or she no longer attends to it (again, a shift in focus of attention). It may be that the patient can relax the muscles involuntarily in order to breathe easier or to "cure" a spastic colon (a physiological change).

The next step is to think of a common, everyday experience that involves the selected physiological change or shift in focus of attention. If the goal is to increase blood flow into the person's hand (e.g., for the treatment of Raynaud's disease or migraine headaches), the therapist may use such analogies as having the hands in warm water, holding them up to a fire, wearing mittens into a warm building in the winter, or holding a date's hand and getting sweaty.

The third step is to connect the analogous experience or understanding to the context of the actual problem. Sometimes, the therapist does this by implication; merely using the analogy while providing therapy or hypnosis for the somatic complaint may be enough to connect the two. At other times, the therapist makes an explicit connection by means of a punchline, as Erickson did in the first case described when he said, "What people don't know, is that they can lose that pain and they don't know that they can lose that ringing in the ears. . . .All of us grow up believing that when you have pain, you must pay attention to it. And believing when you have ringing of the ears that you must keep on hearing it" (Erickson & Rossi, 1979, p. 105).

REFERENCES

Erickson, M.H., & Rossi, E. (1979). *Hypnotic realities: An exploratory casebook*. New York: Irvington.

Haley, J. (1973). *Uncommon therapy: The psychiatric techniques of Milton H. Erickson, M.D.* New York: Norton.

O'Hanlon, B. (1982). Strategic pattern intervention: An integration of individual and family systems therapies based on the work of Milton H. Erickson, M.D. *The Journal of Strategic and Systemic Therapies, 1*(4), 26–33.

O'Hanlon, B., & Wilk, J. (1986). *Shifting contexts: The generation of effective psychotherapy*. New York: Guilford Press.

4

Circular Methods/ Indirect Methods: The Interview As an Indirect Technique

Mary-Jane Ferrier, PhD
Family Institute of Cambridge
Cambridge, Massachusetts

FOR BATESON (1979), TO SPEAK of a dog is to imply, among other things, the existence of bones. He insisted that it is possible to begin to understand the meaning of one thing and communicate about it only in relation to some other thing that is implied by the first. Thus, to speak of *indirect* methods of therapy is to imply that there are *direct* ones.

In the normal course of our lives, we commonly deal in direct approaches. In fact, human beings are fond of telling one another what to do. Local residents give strangers *directions* to the nearest subway stop; accountants and lawyers give their clients direct suggestions on the best way to proceed in various matters. Parents directly tell their children what activities are acceptable. Therapeutic directives for this or that behavior, whether given in a behaviorist's or a structuralist's office, surely qualify as direct in that their intent is to change *directly* a pattern of behavior. Madanes (1984) seemed to suggest that therapists must decide whether to proceed directly or indirectly on the basis of their understanding of the family's or person's attitude toward making the desirable changes (i.e., whether the family will resist the therapist's directives).

PROBLEMS WITH DIRECT METHODS

Those in the field of family therapy who have been influenced by Humberto Maturana find the concept of direct intervention problematic. Maturana (1978) used the term *instructive interaction* to refer to the direct influence of one organism on another that brings about some change in the other. He claimed that

25

instructive interaction does not take place, however, but is a figment of our imaginations or, at best, a not very useful nor very accurate metaphor. According to Maturana, no outside influence can alter an organism, extend its range, increase its possibilities, or make it be or do anything other than what it is and does. In his terms, an organism is autopoietic (i.e., self-producing) or autonomous. This is an uncomfortable position for a therapist to consider; it represents what may be unwelcome "news." At the very least, this position forces therapists to consider what they are about in therapy.

SIMILAR PROBLEMS WITH INDIRECT METHODS

Maturana's position raises questions not only about the validity of *direct* methods in therapy, but also about the validity of *indirect* methods. Maturana appears to insist that *no* outside agent can influence the behavior or development of an autopoietic organism. From a Batesonian perspective, however, the distinction between direct and indirect therapeutic methods does seem to have some validity, although the distinction between them may not be so simple as it first appears. For example, parents who seek therapy because their 10-year-old son wets the bed every night commonly expect the therapist to address that problem explicitly, perhaps by setting up a schedule of reinforcements for the child and involving the parents as dispensers of rewards or keepers of the schedule. Most observers would call that a direct intervention. If, on the other hand, the therapist discerns a pattern of interaction around that problem (e.g., the parents habitually argue over his bedtime just

before he goes to bed), the therapist may suggest what appears to be a very indirect intervention (e.g., one or the other parent should "take a vacation" from the child's bedtime for a while). Thus, the distinction between direct and indirect intervention blurs when levels of analysis are considered.

The distinctions that the observer makes guide the observer's construction of meaning—and so his actions (Bateson, 1979). Another observer, making a different set of distinctions, may consider the therapist's suggestion that one parent take a vacation from the boy's bedtime to be quite direct. Such an observer may view the interaction in terms of the therapist-family system and may believe that the therapist is directly telling the parents to change a pattern of behavior and, therefore, is having a direct impact on the family system.

Therapists must be clear in their mind about the level on which they are working, because effective action is probably always taken at a level different from that on which the family is operating. The distinction between direct and indirect interventions may, in reality, be based on actions taken at different levels of analysis. The Milan Group made it very clear that paradoxical interventions are often formulations that *match* the apparent paradoxes of the family's own interactional patterns and so are paradoxical only from one level of analysis (Selvini-Palazzoli, Boscolo, Cecchin, & Prata, 1978). As paradox may be in the eye of the beholder, so, too, may be indirection.

BASIC NOTIONS OF SYSTEMIC THERAPY

Systemic therapy is based on a set of assumptions about change in human interactional systems (e.g., families). First is the assumption that change is going on all the time. Change is one aspect of a reciprocally related phenomenon that Keeney and Ross (1985) represented as ''stability/change.'' A family changes so that it may remain the same, so that it may retain its identity as *this* family. From this point of view, that which therapists often refer to as ''stuckness '' is a way of changing to remain the same that is unsatisfactory to family members or to someone outside the family whose views are significant. Accordingly, the systemic therapist's goal in therapy is to make it possible for the family's way of changing to change (Tomm, 1984a). Moreover, in the systemic schema, the change that will inevitably take place is *unpredictable*; no therapists or any other observers know how *this* family will actually change its pattern of changing-to-remain-the-same. A therapist cannot lay out a specific plan that includes the how, the where, and the what. Families change in very idiosyncratic ways, arriving at solutions that no one could have fashioned ahead of time.

At the core of systemic therapy is the assumption that there is a reciprocal relationship between belief and behavior. A family's belief in what its members consider good, right, and effective (i.e., ''our way'') guides certain actions. If the actions are successful or satisfactory in one matter, the belief is further validated, and later actions of the same order are likely to be guided by this belief also. In the usual course of events, beliefs are modified by information that enters the belief-behavior loop, and which, in turn, modifies subsequent actions. In this way, families develop flexible interaction patterns that, through multiple fine-tuning

changes, preserve the stability of the family's identity and the stability of the relationships between family members.

When, for whatever reason, useful or relevant information does not enter the belief-behavior loop, the family members may begin to experience difficulties. Without the fine-tuning changes that modify beliefs and subsequent behavior, a wide discrepancy between beliefs and behavior may develop (Tomm, 1984a). The family's beliefs are a set of maps to guide action, but the maps no longer cover the territory at hand. Just as a 1950 map is of no use in finding a town established in 1980, a belief-action sequence that was eminently useful for handling a 10-year-old is no longer useful when the child has reached 13.

Strategic therapists often refer to the behavior patterns that develop around a problem as ''more of the same wrong solution.'' One of the differences, in practice and in theoretical orientation, between this formulation and that of systemic therapists, is their emphasis on the importance of the family's underlying belief system and on behavior-through-time, or history, active in the present. Therapists who have adopted the systemic approach often prescribe different behavior patterns, such as the well-known odd days/even days ritual (Selvini-Palazzoli, Boscolo, Cecchin, & Prata, 1977), but there is always an underlying suggestion of an alternative punctuation of the presently known ''facts'' of the situation. For example, to prescribe treating a child as ''naughty'' one day and ''sick'' the next is to suggest, however covertly, that there are alternative ways of thinking about the child's behavior. The circular interview, perhaps the Milan Group's most important contribution to the practice of family therapy, is based on this very important assumption about beliefs and their role in the development of interactional patterns (Selvini-Palazzoli, Boscolo, Cecchin, & Prata, 1980).

THE CIRCULAR INTERVIEW AS AN INDIRECT METHOD

In reflecting on the implications of Maturana's theories, specifically his contention that there is no such thing as instructive interaction, Efran and Lukens (1985) noted the experience that people have when they go to Disney World:

> In a nutshell, the Disney people (and Maturana) understand that you do not change organisms— you design an environment in which organisms thrive, respond, and *change themselves.* (p. 23)

In a well-conducted circular interview, the therapist and the family do just that— they co-create an environment in which it is possible for new information to enter the family's present established patterns of belief and behavior so that the family can change its current way of changing. As Tomm (1985) noted, "the circular interview is a systemic *enactment* in the relationship between the therapist and the family" (p. 34). By its very nature, it proceeds by *indirection*. The concept of information entering the family members' patterns of belief and behavior follows a Batesonian perspective, the one on which the Milan Group has based its work. A view based on Maturana's notions alone would not include the concept of information entering an autonomous system.

In the circular interview, the therapist adopts the attitude of an explorer in the family members' belief system and the consequent interaction patterns. He or she makes no value judgment on the rights or wrongs of this reality, maintaining at all times a neutral stance and accepting the different views of different family members with equal interest. The criterion for all inquiries, as it is for all hypotheses and interventions, is *usefulness* rather than the pursuit of truth or the rights and wrongs of the situation. Asking questions creates the environment that permits the emergence of differing perspectives, opinions, and beliefs (i.e., news of difference) and, thence, change in the process of change.

In a circular interview, participants become observers of their own reality (Parry, 1984). When the therapist asks one family member to comment on the interactions of two or more others, the others learn how that family member sees and interprets their behaviors. As the therapist goes around the group, knitting together the various observations and checking them against each other, a picture of this family's reality begins to emerge for everyone present. According to Bateson (1979), such a method of double or multiple comparison produces a bonus of meaning that is more than additive. It is somewhat similar to watching the image emerge on a piece of photographic paper in the developer. This circular process makes explicit for the family members opinions and beliefs that had been only surmised or, perhaps, misinterpreted.

A family sought therapy because the mother had repeatedly attempted suicide. She was apparently considered by the family and by the helping network to be seriously depressed or "sad," as the family had described it.

Therapist: Before your mother tries to kill herself and then goes to the hospital, what do you suppose she is thinking?

Son: She gets very sad and cries a lot. No one can make her come out of it. She won't let anyone near her.

Therapist: Is there anyone in the family who can get near her then?

Son: No. . . .

Therapist: (to daughter) Do you agree with your brother that, when your mother won't let anyone near her, she is more sad, like someone who lost a loved one, for example, or do you suppose she is more angry about something?

Daughter: (slowly) I sometimes wonder if she isn't mad at my father sometimes because he won't let her go back to work.

In such an exchange, the other members of the family hear a piece of "news" from the daughter—the discrepancy between what had appeared to be a commonly held belief about the situation and this novel interpretation of it.

A single fragment in itself may not be a significant piece of news, but the accumulation of such fragments with their introduction of different opinions about familiar, unexamined patterns increases the complexity of the family's field of attention and so creates the potential for news of difference that makes a difference. The therapist offers no *direct* suggestions or interventions in the conduct of such an interview. The therapist's practice of neutrality precludes such actions (Selvini-Palazzoli et al., 1980).

Therapists do make many indirect suggestions to families in a circular inter-view. The fact that the structure of the interview has been imposed by the therapist's hypotheses is an indirect suggestion that there are a variety of ways in which to examine the same "facts." This in itself is a powerful piece of "news" for families that have come to therapy with severely limited strategies for dealing with their problems and a seeming inability to consider other options. The circular exploration in which the therapist actively solicits each person's opinion and accepts each one as valid is usually a very different experience for the family members and implicitly suggests a complexity in their problems of which they are unaware.

In addition, the therapist often uses what Tomm has called "reflexive questions" (Tomm, 1985). Essentially, these marginally neutral questions bear within themselves an embedded suggestion that is a little more subtle, perhaps, than the old question "When did you stop beating your wife?" Certainly, the question addressed to the daughter in the dialogue carried within it the suggestion that the mother's reason for not letting anyone near her might very well be something other than sadness, such as anger. The function of such questions is similar to that of more elaborate or discursive reframes—they offer another way to conceptualize the situation. When a meaning changes, so can behaviors, and vice versa. Family members deal with an angry mother differently than they deal with a sad one.

A SPECIAL CASE OF INDIRECTION IN SYSTEMIC METHODOLOGY

From time to time, individuals seek therapy for what they see as a family problem.

It is more common, however, for individuals to seek help around a problem that they consider "personal" or somehow within themselves, even though they may talk about difficulties with others (e.g., spouses, friends, children, bosses). Just as many families believe that their problems reside within one of their members, many individuals believe that their problems reside primarily within themselves rather than in the system of which they are a part. The therapist's insistence on the presence of family members at sessions is itself a powerful intervention in the family's epistemology. Family attendance at therapy sessions dramatizes a way of thinking about their situation that is different from their usual conceptualizations.

When an individual seeks therapy, the therapist can ask for the attendance of other members of that person's family. This is not always feasible, however, and the therapist's repeated requests can lead to symmetrical struggles over control of who attends. Moreover, it may not be necessary. Provided that the therapist thinks about problems in a systemic framework, builds hypotheses of a systemic nature, and conducts interviews with a systemic approach, the individual will be face to face with a novel way of considering the problem. In short, such an approach bears within itself the potential for being news of difference (Ferrier, in press).

A young woman sought therapy because, as she said, "everything was up in the air" for her. She had been flitting from one thing to another ever since she had graduated from college 4 years before, had never had a real job, aspired to be an artist but had never progressed beyond the point of dabbling, and had ended a relationship with a boyfriend a few months earlier. In addition, she was financially dependent on her parents. She reported that she had been depressed ever since the breakup with her boyfriend and had been suicidal a few months ago. This young woman had been in psychotherapy several times before and clearly expected that treatment would focus on her own inner experience. At the first session, she was prepared to tell the therapist all about her current feelings, especially about her sense of helplessness and depression.

Not far into that first session, the therapist had formed the initial impression that here was a young woman who perceived herself as flawed and in need of some sort of "repair" so that she could get on with her life. In the therapist's head there was a competing paradigmatic hypothesis: there was a significant network out there (her family?) within which this young woman's behavior would make sense. Accordingly, the therapist began to shift the focus of the interview into more relational terms, using the suicidal thoughts as the point of departure for an exploration of the significant network.

Therapist: Who was the first person to know that you wanted to kill yourself last fall?

Client: Well, . . . I talked with my sister. She was very worried, but . . . I guess . . . she knew that if I told her—I must be really OK.

Therapist: You mean . . .

Client: . . . that if I could talk about it, I wasn't going to do it.

Therapist: When you told your sister, did you want her to keep it a secret or tell someone else?

Client: I didn't want my mother to know. Her best friend's daughter killed herself last summer. She'd be hurt. She freaked out.

Therapist: Would she be surprised you had been thinking of killing yourself?

Client: Not really. . . . I think it would really hurt her. She wants me to be happy . . . whatever she can do . . . she wants to help out.

Therapist: If she found out you were unhappy, she'd be hurt . . . because she'd failed you, or because you hadn't told her?

Client: More that she had failed me. It just saddens her too much.

Therapist: Do you think your father was worried about you?

Client: He acted real funny this year—super friendly.

Therapist: And that wasn't typical?

Client: Not so typical. We get along when we're not on their turf . . . when we're traveling. Otherwise, we never deal on an adult level. When I visit them, my father doesn't communicate much—he doesn't show emotion or anything—he's real insecure. He'd just shuffle around the house being quiet, and my mother would be real tense, not knowing what to say.

Therapist: How would you know if your father were worried about you?

Client: When he's really been worried, he's been more open. He's actually come up and hugged me when I arrived at the house—to show me he cares.

Therapist: When that happens . . . it sounds like it takes a lot to make him show he really cares. . . .

Client: I feel like they've been talking (*laughs*).

Therapist: Does that make you then more worried about yourself . . . because then you know how serious it is . . . ?

Client: I feel like I'm really a sicky now.

The relationship information packed into this short exchange enabled the therapist to begin to put flesh on the paradigmatic hypothesis that had guided the inquiry so far. Moreover, it was becoming evident from her responses to the therapist's questions that the client was becoming intrigued by the process itself. The session continued in this vein.

Aged 26, the client was the youngest of three children. She had a 30-year-old sister and a 28-year-old brother. All three were still semidependent on their parents; until recently, none appeared to have made any solid commitments to work or to relationships outside the family. Within the last year, however, the sister had entered into a relationship that looked as if it might become a longlasting commitment—even though the parents did not approve.

By the end of the second session, the therapist had formulated and explored the hypothesis that the client, as the youngest in the family, either was attempting to move into or was being drawn into the emotional space being vacated by her elder sister. In a sense, her depression and lack of direction maintained the balance in the overall family, distracting the parents from the "loss" of the elder sister. She so worried them that they "talked together" as she put it, and her father rallied from his own somewhat depressive, withdrawn behavior ("shuffling around the house") to show his affection for her. At the end of the second session, she was given a question to ask her great aunt, who had emerged in the exploration as the family observer and commentator across several generations: "What do you think will happen in my parents' relationship when all three of us kids finally grow up?"

At the beginning of the third session, the client reported that she had talked not only with her great aunt, but also with an aunt by marriage, the wife of her mother's brother. Both aunts had said that they thought the parents would be OK.

Therapist: If you had asked them, "Would my parents be more like good friends or more like lovers?" what do you suppose they would have said?

Client: They're at the good friends stage—maybe more romantic than we know.

Therapist: Your aunt is more their generation—closer to their age— what do you suppose she'd say?

Client: It would be nice . . . she'd probably say they'd be good friends . . . 'cause that's what she'd know. But it's possible they could be lovers.

Therapist: If you'd asked your great aunt?

Client: Friends . . . friends . . . they have that going for them anyway!

Therapist: Did you ask anyone else— you said . . .

Client: I talked to Jane [her best friend] about it. I just told her how excited I was because of this new idea that they are hanging on for a reason because they can't let go— in case the marriage might fall apart—they'd have to face things they've been avoiding. She thought it was a great idea. . . I mean a great question . . . she didn't really . . .

Therapist: She didn't have an opinion . . . ?

Client: Not really—it was a sort of rush telephone conversation.

Therapist: What do *you* think would happen?

Client: Well, when you first asked me, I thought, O my God, they don't want to give up us kids because they don't want to face how their present relationship might be and . . .

Therapist: So you immediately thought of it as maybe a negative thing. . . .

Client: First—initially, I thought it would be—a good explanation of why they are acting the way they are. They don't *want* to get rid of the kids. Then I thought—What would they have without us? Would they have a marriage—a workable marriage? And I'm sure they'd stick it out. There wouldn't be any reason for divorce. They're not the type that would. And that's also what other people's reactions were . . . looking at it in terms of would the marriage continue. But I don't think that's so much an issue.

The client's opinion of the current status of her parents' relationship and its future if she and her siblings were to get on with their own lives never became crystal clear. Toward the end of this interview, however, she announced that she had decided to take a job in another state where she would have the opportunity to enroll in graduate school. This was an idea she had toyed with for some time, but she had not been ready to act on it before.

Although there was no dramatic turnaround in this woman's life, something had happened in the course of a few short weeks that had made it possible for her to entertain new options and to act on them. The sessions themselves had been a novel experience for her. The questions had so intrigued her that she had taken not only the one given to her by the therapist, but also others into her network to share with other people who were significant to her. The examination of her helplessness and depression within the context of this network had offered her a view of her reality that was different from the one that she had originally brought to therapy and, with that view, had given her new meanings for her own behavior.

From the very beginning, this therapy was conducted according to a systemic conceptualization and a circular methodology. At no time did the therapist offer any direct advice, make any suggestions, or offer any opinion about the various views of the problem that were elicited by the questions. True, the question that the client was given to ask her great aunt was similar to an embedded suggestion question, thus representing a covert opinion of the therapist. The entire interview process was one of indirection, however. The therapist's initial paradigmatic hypothesis framed the interviews in a wider reality, placing this woman's problems squarely within an interactional pattern with which she was so familiar that she was virtually unaware of it. Like the fish, she became aware of the sea in which she swam and of the other fish who shared it with her. Apparently, this experience prompted her to explore another part of the ocean.

SOME TENTATIVE CONCLUSIONS

In systemic work with individuals, as indeed with families and couples, the clients, observe their own behavior and make one set of distinctions that specifies the way in which "the problem" is perceived and, in turn, leads to a certain set of actions. The systemic therapist makes a different set of distinctions—takes the same "facts" and places them in a different, systemic frame. Moreover, with this different set of distinctions comes the possibility of seeing the *relationship* between "facts" (e.g., actions, people) from a different perspective. Indeed, the wider view may bring into focus connecting patterns that could not be seen before and so could have no meaning for the client.

In the process of facilitating the exploration of this systemic reality, therapists validate many alternative ways of responding to events, to circumstances, and to people by means of their neutral stance. This neutrality flows from the original distinctions that they have made (i.e., the basic assumptions of the systemic view) about how belief and behavior interact, how they develop, and how they change. This view is usually an alternative view and, thus, a novel one for clients. As Kuhn (1970) observed with regard to scientific revolutions, once there has been a reorganization of the "data," it is a different universe that the scientist observes. In systemic therapy, the goal is to make it possible for clients to reorganize the "data" of their experience.

Maturana's ideas continue to raise serious questions about the effect of any outside influence on the beliefs or behavior of an individual or a family, whether the methods used in an effort to exert that influence are direct or indirect. The proc-ess described in this discussion does seem to proceed by indirection, in the sense that there is no attempt to take direct action to influence the client in one particular way. The therapist accepts the inevitability of change, but acknowledges that the manner and the direction will be unpredictable. Maturana's notions raise the inevitable question: If therapists are in the business of change, what are they doing when they are doing therapy? In a circular interview, a therapist is attempting to co-create with clients a richer, more complex environment in which they can choose to change themselves in their own idiosyncratic, unpredictable ways.

REFERENCES

Bateson, G. (1972). *Steps to an ecology of mind.* New York: Ballantine Books.

Bateson, G. (1979). *Mind and nature: A necessary unity.* New York: Dutton.

Efran, J., & Lukens, M. (1985). The world according to Humberto Maturana. *The Family Therapy Networker, 9*(3), 23–28.

Ferrier, M-J. (in press). Testing the limits in Milan systemic therapy: Working with an individual. In D. Efron (Ed.), *Developments in strategic and systemic therapy.* New York: Brunner/Mazel.

Keeney, B.P., & Ross, J.M. (1985). *Mind in therapy: Constructing systemic family therapies.* New York: Basic Books.

Kuhn, T. (1970). *The structure of scientific revolutions: International encyclopedia of science* (Vol. 2). Chicago: University of Chicago Press.

Madanes, C. (1984). *Behind the one-way mirror.* San Francisco: Jossey-Bass.

Maturana, H. (1978). Biology of language: The epistemology of reality. In G. Miller (Ed.), *Psychology and biology of language and thought* (pp. 27–63). New York: Academic Press.

Parry, A. (1984). The maturanation of Milan: Recent developments in systemic therapy. *Journal of Strategic and Systemic Therapies, 3*(1), 35–42.

Selvini-Palazzoli, M., Boscolo, L., Cecchin, G., & Prata, G. (1977). Family rituals: A powerful tool in family therapy. *Family Process, 16*(4), 445–453.

Selvini-Palazzoli, M., Boscolo, L., Cecchin, G., & Prata, G. (1978). *Paradox and counterparadox: A new model in the therapy of the family in schizophrenic transaction.* New York: Jason Aronson.

Selvini-Palazzoli, M., Boscolo, L., Cecchin, G., & Prata, G. (1980). Hypothesizing-circularity-neutrality: Three guidelines for the conductor of the session. *Family Process, 19,* 3–12.

Tomm, K. (1984a). One perspective on the Milan systemic approach: Part I. *Journal of Marital and Family Therapy, 10*(2), 113–125.

Tomm, K. (1984b). One perspective on the Milan systemic approach: Part II. *Journal of Marital and Family Therapy, 10*(3), 253–271.

Tomm, K. (1985). Circular interviewing: A multifaceted clinical tool. In D. Campbell & R. Draper (Eds.), *Applications of systemic family therapy: The Milan approach (complementary frameworks of theory and practice)* (pp. 33–45). New York: Grune & Stratton.

5

Exploring Relationships between Ericksonian Hypnotherapy and Family Therapy

Michele K. Ritterman, PhD
Oakland, California

FAMILY THERAPY MODELS have proliferated over the last 30 years. The various theories and techniques for helping troubled families have been compared in terms of such features as symptoms treated, unit of focus of treatment, efficacy, and duration (Green & Framo, 1981). Although a great deal has been discovered about the ways in which feelings and behaviors circulate through the developing family organism, much remains to be learned. For example, it is known that family members can alter each other's blood chemistry (Minuchin, Rosman, & Baker, 1978), but how? In distinguishing themselves from individual therapists, family therapists have often placed internal or interior phenomena in the background of study and treatment, regarding them as derivatives of family structure.

Erickson's work has also multiplied, producing offshoots that link it to both individual-based psychotherapies (Lankton & Lankton, 1983) and family therapy (Calof, 1985; Haley, 1963; Lankton & Lankton, 1983; Ritterman, 1983). The Ericksonian therapist typically works outward from the inside of an individual—the opposite of the family therapist in the direction of change. Erickson helped individuals to rearrange their interior reality before they ventured forth to change their relational landscape.

Obviously, an individual's family context—the object of study of family therapists—and the individual's context of mind—the primary interest of hypnotists—stand in some relationship to one another; both may be tributaries to the stream of symptomatic behaviors. If the symptom bearer's habitual sequences of thought and commonly accessible states of mind are considered one level of his functioning, while the patterns and structural alignments of his family are considered another, related level of his functioning, it appears that Ericksonian hypnotherapists and the structural and strategic therapists may be examining similar processes and intervening at opposite ends of the problem sequence: family therapists working from the outside, inward; Ericksonian therapists working from the inside, outward.

Erickson assumed that behavior changes brought about by changes in the patient's internal associative maps will catalyze new reactions in familial or broader social contexts; this process may be called exteriorization. Family therapists, on the other hand, use a process that may be called interiorization; changes in the family—in the roles of one or more family members; in the feeling, tone, or ambience of family life; in the spoken and unspoken rules that govern distributions of power and units of responsibility within the family bureaucracy—spark in individual members new behaviors that, in turn, catalyze rearrangements within the individuals' unconscious associative maps as well.

Human phenomena seem sufficiently complex that working from the outside, inward, while simultaneously working from the inside, outward, may be useful. It may be that synthesizing understandings from these two orientations will make it possible to affect symptom cycles from both sides of the dialectic, approaching symptoms through several openings, transforming them, and recoding of experience across levels.

In addition to recognition of these cross-level relationships, there are other similarities between these therapies. For example, it is assumed in both that the symptom is neither the true problem nor an expression of psychiatric illness, but rather a metaphorical expression of a problem and an attempt at resolution. In this sense, therapists seek and salvage benevolent aspects of symptoms (Madanes, 1981; Ritterman, 1983). Also, the underlying problem is understood to be inflexibly patterned behavior resulting from internal and/or interactional rules that proscribe available choices and prevent the resolution of developmentally routine or unusual life dilemmas. The emphasis in therapy is on setting up circumstances, interior or exterior, that enable the patient to alter the rules and look through a new opening to an expanded range of ideation, emotion, and interaction.

Each of these therapies promotes a responsible and directive stance on the part of the therapist as change agent. Nevertheless, they share a penchant for indirection in technique. In order to intervene *directly* with an *indirectly* (metaphorically) expressed dilemma, these therapists use stories, metaphors, ambiguous or humorous tasks, ordeals, and other rituals in therapy (Haley, 1984; Madanes, 1981; Minuchin, 1974).

It is important to identify similarities and differences between these approaches in order to explore the point of convergence *between* individual and collective, unconscious and interpersonal events and to develop understandings that encompass themes common to both sides of the existential dialectic.

PRODUCING CHANGE WITHIN RIGID PATTERNS

Erickson's Focus on Interior Patterns and States of Mind

One of Erickson's contributions to the field of psychotherapy has been his demonstration that each human mind— inclusive of all related cognitive, affective, motor, kinesthetic, perceptual, and physiological behavior—is a unique and underutilized resource. His life work was characterized by his interest in activating special capacities of the mind, particularly those common in trance states, and in helping people use those capacities to solve problems in living. The discovery of a patient's range of mental states and mental-behavioral potentials were synonymous with treatment in Ericksonian hypnotherapy.

Erickson directed his therapeutic energies toward helping patients to collect useful memories and ideas scattered or repressed throughout their belief systems and to integrate those into a new set of beliefs or state of consciousness, complete with physiological and interactional components. He also helped patients mobilize already intact hidden psychological states and sequences of thinking. Hypnosis was central to his therapy because it converted the unconscious from a source of resistance into a resource in this creative process. The patients' understandings gained through hypnosis made it easier for Erickson to establish the necessarily intense rapport with them and to make suggestions acceptable to the patients despite the fact that their typical sequences of thought or states of consciousness were being challenged.

Erickson recognized that family life cycle problems and social difficulties could be transformed and recoded into frequently repeating memories and beliefs within an individual's mindset (Haley, 1973). His individual therapy drew power from its focus on interiorized family life cycle phenomena as they

manifested themselves in the order and arrangement of memories, associations, and ideas or in certain limiting states of mind. Often, his therapy bulwarked individuals against the destructive powers that distressing social circumstance held over them. In this sense, Erickson worked to break the spell of a dysfunctional relational rapport via the symptom bearer's behavioral patterns (Ritterman, 1985).

A young woman who had adopted her family's ambience of despair as her prevailing state of mind was challenged to scan her memory in trance, collecting bits of sensation and feeling to produce and sustain an alternative state of mind. As a result, she developed a heightened curiosity that allowed her to respond to her family and others in new ways (M. Erickson, personal communication, 1976).

Erickson held that individuals with a symptom were constricted by their own certainties, their own rules, whether these rules guided their belief system, their perceptions of self, their patterns of physiological response or relational habits, or their own ideas of contingency, (i.e., if A, then B). Certainly, symptomatic patients who have closely followed their conscious and unconscious maps may understandably feel lost. Their very system of logic precludes the kind of curious questioning that permits expanded experience and new understandings such as, why bother with A, and what about B *in this context*? Erickson had little interest in the content of a person's problem per se, but was greatly interested in what a piece of information revealed about the rigidities in a person's belief system, mindsets, and relations to family and community.

Erickson often demonstrated to patients and students how insufferably rigid their own mindsets were by confronting them with "a simple puzzle, for anyone with reasonable intelligence":

> A farmer plants five rows of trees, four trees in each row, ten trees total. How is that possible? (M. Erickson, personal communication, 1976)*

Schooling and social patterns lead individuals to think along certain lines automatically; once an alternative line of thought has been recognized, however, this puzzle is readily solved. In the same way, replacing a limiting sequence of ideas with other architectures of consciousness opens the way for the spontaneous expression of little used capacities and the emergence of new feelings, responses, and ideas.

Erickson's strategy of treatment was based on finding an idiosyncratic way to help a patient scale the walls of such limitations:

> In the initial interview, the therapist gathers the relevant facts regarding the patient's problems and the repertory of life experiences and learnings that will be utilized for therapeutic purposes. Patients have problems because of learned limitations. They are caught in mental sets, frames of reference, and belief systems that do not permit them to explore and utilize their own abilities to best advantage. Human beings are still in the process of learning to use their potentials. The therapeutic transaction ideally creates a new phenomenal world in which patients can explore their potentials, freed to some extent from their learned limitations. . . . Therapeutic trance is a period during which patients are able to break out of their limited frameworks and belief systems so they can experience other patterns of functioning within themselves. (Erickson & Rossi, 1980, p. 2)

A man well-known in his field was required to pass an oral examination before he could be licensed; he had failed so many times previously that he was permitted only one more attempt to pass (M. Erickson, personal communication, 1977). Not only was this the man's last chance, but also his enemy in the field, one of the few professionals who disliked him, was to be his examiner. He contacted Erickson. Because Erickson had no doubt that the man knew his material, he surmised that anxiety interfered with the man's performance on the test. Other therapies had focused on such issues as the man's relationship with his father, unconscious anger, and fear of male authority, but these therapies had failed.

Recognizing "unconscious resistance," nevertheless, Erickson looked at the case more pragmatically. He spent the therapy hours training the man in deep trance to use a wide variety of hypnotic phenomena, including positive and negative hallucinations, amnesias, and visualization. The goal was to help the man (1) enter a different, more positively charged state of consciousness than he had used in the earlier examinations and (2) use his special deep trance capacities to change his patterns of thought and action.

As Erickson had taught him, the man automatically went into a deep

---

*Puzzle solution: The rows are in the shape of a five-pointed star; they are not parallel.

trance state—unrecognizable as such to others—when he went into the oral examination. Although he knew the direction from which his nemesis' voice came, he used his skill with negative hallucination to "not-see" the face of his examiner, which might otherwise have frightened him. The examiner asked him a question so long that, under ordinary circumstances, even recall of the question would have been difficult. The man used a positive hallucination to see every word as if it were typed out before his eyes, however, and was able to read and reread the question until he had a thorough grasp of it. In this way, the man took and passed the examination. As a result of his private hypnosis training with Erickson, he was able to develop his own autoimmune responses in defense against previously overriding anxiety.

Minuchin's Focus on Exterior Patterns and Family Structures

Like Erickson, Minuchin uses rigid patterning as his primary point of therapeutic entry. In his case, however, arrangements that shape family interactions are focal. As Erickson moved into the interior realities that order a person's life, Minuchin probes the "extracerebral mind" of the symptom bearer (Minuchin, 1974).

Minuchin defines a patient's problem within the context of the multibodied family organism. Family conflict manifests itself in various ways, such as children and grandmother versus single mother; father and grandmother versus mother and son; mother and daughter versus father; or mother versus father in

chronic parenting conflict. Minuchin broadens his lens to obtain the wide-angle view, searching for a troubled pattern of interaction, complete with unhelpful rules of alignment and bothersome sets of interactional patterns. He looks for the most tangible representation of the whole family problem and organizes a session around it. The symptom is an ulcer in the family body. It is the signal of a wound in the chest wall. It is an outcry from the family lung, too stifled to breathe freely.

The oldest brother in a family returned home from a high-level position abroad with a depression and a wish to be dead. Minuchin learned that the man—who was treated as the family failure—was a rich and successful banker, supporting his father and his father's family for several years during the father's near-bankruptcy (S. Minuchin, personal communication, 1974). The troubled young man was both metaphorically and literally wearing his father's old shoes, however. In a family interview, Minuchin had the young man remove his shoes, wrap them in his father's newspaper, and leave barefoot. He was told to go barefoot until he was standing in his own shoes.

Implicit in this directive was the idea that the young man could not be developmentally healthy when he was playing at being his father (apparently a thankless job) and literally standing in his father's shoes.

Often Minuchin gives every family member a task that is complementary to rigidities and ambiguities in the family's interactional rule system. As the whole family reconstructs bits and pieces or rules about the boundaries of the various subsystems (e.g., spousal, parental, or sibling), the family creates a new ambience, activates new possibilities for greater distance or intimacy, and draws closer to the next stage of family development.

Minuchin reads rigidified family structure by means of a process that he calls "mapping" (Minuchin, 1974). The symptoms of the index patient are regarded as components of rigidly repeating transactional sequences that are momentarily frozen in a characteristic structure. In order to disrupt this symptom-sustaining structure, the therapist may intervene at any point(s) in the structure.

The self-esteem of the young man who had been father to his father was very low; this was partly the cause and partly the effect of his family's perception of him as the family failure. He was trapped in a family structure with his father and younger brother in which he played the role of inadequate, bumbling son. In Minuchin's diagrammatic representation of family structure, a map of this family structure would look as follows:

Instead of focusing on the subject of their discussion, Minuchin looked for a moment in which all three men were playing their role and introduced a challenge to the structural arrangement. At one point, after listening to the father and the younger son talk as equals, he turned to the symptomatic man and said, "Why is it your younger brother speaks to your father in sentences, and you must always use paragraphs?" The question was designed to loosen an alignment by capturing the behavior of the banker—in this case, his indecisive rambling—that made him a failure relative to his brother and father.

Whatever the subject, the clinical contents are used to help the therapist intervene in the underlying structure or arrangement. Both context and sequences of communication are important, because they reveal the structural rules that shape them. The therapist works to establish new alignments that can be generalized, transforming a wide range of problem contents.

A hallmark of Minuchin's approach—as characteristic of his work as trance is characteristic of Erickson's—is his use of the therapeutic context for the enact-

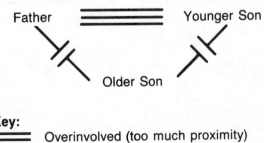

Key:

⬛ Overinvolved (too much proximity)

⊣⊢ Distant (or peripheral)

ment of typical family interactional patterns, as well as for the enactment of intense, sustained, structurally corrective experiences. Just as Erickson used a patient's own patterns to establish a new hypnotic reality, Minuchin uses common, everyday interactions to produce a working reality.

Minuchin's description of the therapeutic result of changing family communication routes is similar to Erickson's description of the therapeutic result of loosening rigid mindsets. Minuchin emphasizes that the rigid structures operative at the onset of therapy are not the only ones in a family's repertoire. At any time, a family may be trapped within a narrow range of contractual arrangements, however. Other, less used structures or ways of organizing family activity may, if induced, permit more desirable functioning. Family structure changes may promote new or less prominent family connections, allowing new aspects of individual personality to unfold. This is the other pole of the Ericksonian dialectic; "changed organization makes possible a continuous reinforcement of the changed experience, which provides a validation of the changed sense of self" (Minuchin, 1974, pp. 13–14).

DIRECTION, INDIRECTION, AND UTILIZATION

Common to Ericksonian hypnotherapy and strategic family therapy are the principles of therapist responsibility for the course of therapy and indirection within the therapeutic process. Haley pioneered several explorations of power exchanges within the therapist-patient relationship (Haley, 1963). Observation and experi-

ence taught him that therapists are most effective when responsibly in charge of the therapeutic course.

In one case supervision, Haley told the therapist that she had behaved during a family interview as if she were unable to turn her head from the mother. Indeed, she had stared at the mother with a vacant kind of look, her head bobbing up and down perseveratively, and had never looked at other family members, even if they spoke to her. "The mother has you in a trance," he said (Haley, personal communication, 1974).

This is not to say that a therapist cannot use this "other" state of consciousness in observing and understanding family dynamics. In fact, a family induction of the therapist often offers clues to the way in which the symptom bearer is influenced. When the therapist is inadvertently or routinely put into a trance by the family, however, or fails to awaken better informed for the reverie, the therapist may not be in charge of the therapy. According to Haley, the therapist who is not in charge is likely to be organized by the family and induced to sustain its unhelpful patterns.

Erickson, too, emphasized that the therapist must take charge of the therapeutic course. He noted that the way to be helpfully in charge is to observe carefully and respond in kind to information that patients provide about their particular difficulty. This scrutiny, at conscious and unconscious levels, reveals the patient's arrangements of thought and action and identifies the door that is open for therapeutic entry.

Erickson's Interest in Interior Codes

Shakespeare is not the only person who would advise, ''By indirection find direction out'' (*Macbeth*). Erickson emphasized that it is important for the therapist to speak in the language of the patient. He asserted that all language (i.e., body, verbal, physiological) is coded and that the symptom is itself coded with a wealth of personal associations, many of which will remain unknown to the therapist. Patients cannot or will not talk about their problem more directly. If they could, they might not have the symptom. For example, a patient may complain of a pain in the neck. This ''pain'' may be a statement about abuse from the patient's spouse, parent, child, or boss; it may be an anniversary pain associated with an otherwise forgotten traumatic event; it may represent guilt over the loss of an heirloom that a relative had given the patient; it may be related to whiplash; or it may refer at once to many problems.

Erickson recognized that there are many points of entry into the experiential life of a patient and that, by working on one level (e.g., intrapsychically), the therapist can have an impact on the family life cycle; by affecting the metaphor-rich symptom, the therapist can help the patient to transform and recode new experiential learnings. In fact, the best and most direct way of speaking to patients is to use their own idiosyncratic code. This approach has been called Erickson's indirect form of suggestion. By speaking in the patients' code, the therapist begins to bypass their ordinary patterns of behavior and enter their private inner reality.

Speaking to a patient in code is like speaking to a patient who is in a formally induced trance in that, while the process appears indirect, the communication has an immediacy that is not present in more analytical communication. From the patient's perspective, communication with a hypnotist who is speaking in his or her code, especially while the patient is in trance, is the most direct form of communication that the patient has ever experienced. It is akin to having the hypnotist in the subject's dream, or to having one's bodily processes spoken to.

One suicidal woman justified her attempts in terms of her having a "bad body—a body that was always 'sad' and didn't work right." She said that she had never felt that anyone really understood her until the moment she was spoken to in her code in trance. She wrote of the experience months later:

> I feel like I am in a huge balloon. . . . And nobody can get inside nor can I get out because my feelings are blocking the entrance. Only once someone has come inside, that's you! For just a short while. (Ritterman, 1983, p. 276)

The mysteries of how a hypnotist speaks to the rate of respiration or peristalsis; to the blood supply of a wart on the face, but not the wart hidden between the toes; or to psychophysiological systems that affect the vomiting reflex, breast development, menstrual cycles, or childbirth can best be approached with a recognition that the coded language of the hypnotist speaks directly, intimately, and intensely to the part of the patient's mind that has the most power over the general ordering of feelings, sensations, and ideas.

A hallmark of Erickson's "utilization" therapy (Erickson & Rossi, 1980) was his unrelenting belief that the therapeutic approach must fit the client; the client's heel is not to be cut off to squeeze her foot into some theoretical glass slipper. It is through coded communication that the patient shows the therapist how and when the best response can be obtained. The therapist leads by carefully following the benevolent aspects of these edicts.

Haley's Interest in Exterior Codes

Haley sees in many symptoms an analogous statement about relational problems. According to Haley, a symptom is a coded referent to other problems in family organization, a metaphorical account of a patient's social situation. A wife who vomits at approximately 5:30 each evening—20 minutes before her husband arrives home from work—may be communicating "You disgust me." A child who cannot stand up when her father leaves town may be representing her mother's trouble in standing up (without leaning excessively on the child) while the father is out of town. The metaphor of the symptom is enlarged to reflect patterns of troubled multiperson communications, as well as patterns of individual functioning.

Haley described the case of a young girl whom he called Anabelle (Haley, 1980). During the crisis that initiated therapy, Anabelle suffered a delusion that she was pregnant with multiple children, twins. She was troubled to think she would need an abortion and said that she would sacrifice herself by suicide should her parents separate and abandon their children.

After Anabelle's successful treatment, her mother sought brief therapy for herself before she divorced her husband. In that therapy, the mother revealed that she had been depressed because she had had one child after another (multiple children) and that, although she might have wanted an abortion, she never had one because of her religious beliefs (concern about abortion). She felt that she had wasted her entire life in an uptight marriage (sacrificed herself for her family).

Clearly, the symptom of a child—including thoughts and ideas—can be an analogous statement about the problems of another family member or a reflection of broader family concerns.

Madanes (1981) carries this idea of an individual symptom as a metaphor for family conflicts a step further, saying that the interaction sequences in which the symptom behaviors are embedded are analogous to interaction sequences around other issues. Her strategic rituals and "pretend" interventions correspond to these observable sequences, much as Erickson's hypnotic patterns matched his patient's privately coded communication patterns (Madanes, 1984). Just as Erickson's inner work is preparatory for desirable external consequences, so Haley and Madanes emphasize that no intervention is made before the family members are prepared to be receptive to it.

INTERIORIZATION AND EXTERIORIZATION

Recoding of Family Interactions into Inner Realities

In their classic study of superlabile diabetic children, Minuchin, Rosman, and

Baker (1978) dramatically illustrated how interactionally coded sequences are "interiorized" by the index patient to produce a symptom. In the study, each member of a family had an intravenous blood-sampling unit attached to his or her arm. As the index patient watched from behind a mirror, the therapist activated the type of parental conflict that was believed to stress the child—given his biophysiological predisposition—to the point of illness. The child was then taken to join his parents, who had not resolved their intense conflict. During the process, blood samples were taken from each family member and the concentration of free fatty acids in each sample determined. In this way, a measure of family structure in motion, at the level of blood chemistry, could be taken.

Alterations in the concentration of free fatty acids indicated a danger point for the diabetic child and a shift in the anxiety level of each parent. It was found that the presence of the symptom-bearing child decreased the parents' emotional arousal level automatically, but this decrease in the level of parental stress (without resolution of the original conflict) was at the somatic expense of a continued rise in the child's arousal level that propelled him toward disease.

This research suggests that the structure of the family is coded in the physiological language of its members. Although it does not capture the subtleties of this language, the research demonstrates that family interaction and family ambience affect internal physiological communication. It exposes one facet of the mysterious relationship between seemingly automatic interior phenomena and exterior patterns of family life. The process of interiorization of externally manifested communication sequences is itself neutral, and is as characteristic of the healing process as of symptom production. If destructive family patterns can be translated at cue into private psychophysiological codes (symptom activation), positive versions can also be translated into codes that enhance efficacy in problem solving.

Exteriorization of Internal Events through Action

Erickson did not regard trance states, intact states of mind, hypnotic phenomena, or any other individual psychophysiological capabilities as simply derivatives of life situations. Certainly, context and circumstance can narrow the range of accessible psychological capabilities, but just as certainly mindsets and capabilities associated with special states can be creatively mobilized to override many difficult external arrangements.

In a sense, Erickson examined the universe from the microcosm of the individual patient's mind. When Erickson called in the spouse, parent, or child of a patient, his interest was principally in the impact of that family member on the experience and understandings of the symptom bearer or in that family member as an individual. Whether using subtleties of speech, manipulations of word meanings, body movements, intonation, challenges, or humor in therapy, he was generally less concerned with sequences of interaction *between* the symptom bearer and other family members than with the associative processes activated *within* them. He focused on the *interior* subjective world of the patient, including "hypnotic realities." In this sense, Erickson focused on each individual's margin of personal freedom from any context.

Erickson helped patients broaden the range of mental capabilities that they could use to solve their problems. When conscious linear or descriptive discussion of a problem did not suffice, he used coded and hypnotic communications. Erickson employed trance to help patients

1. bypass ordinary and rigid frames of reference

2. construct alternative mental states

3. activate and bring under their control abilities and skills characteristic of trance, such as

- subjective time distortion, amnesia, and other psychological capabilities
- positive and negative hallucination, and other perceptual capabilities
- dissociation, catalepsy, and other physiological capabilities

He then helped the individual to reify these abilities in acting on external circumstances, including relationships. In fact, Erickson repeatedly confirmed that, once a patient's mindset or a pivotal aspect of his experiential life has been affected, the patient is spontaneously more receptive to many new experiences. "Heartened by the possibility of change, no matter how small, positive or negative, a patient will automatically seek others" (M. Erickson, personal communication, 1976).

Erickson often targeted a feature of the patient's mindset that reflected a conflict in the patient's exterior reality. Therefore, when changes were "triggered" in

the individual, the "bang" was often heard in the broader social context (i.e., the family and other social units).

An enuretic girl had for years suffered from every imaginable psychological, medical, and family intrusion for her problem (M. Erickson, personal communication, 1978). Erickson incorporated this external factor in a novel way in his work with the girl. Using hypnosis, he taught the girl to imagine that, just when she pulled down her pants, sat down on the toilet, and began to urinate, she saw someone at the door. This approach not only encouraged her to use her own natural reflex of constricting the urethra when someone is watching, but also put the ghosts of her intrusive family to good purposes. She used their intrusion, as she imagined it in her trances, to help her activate the needed self-controlling reflex. The physiological control that she gained in this manner enhanced her power over her own problem, her parents, and even over medical science. Other changes in the girl's self-esteem and attitude occurred "spontaneously." Erickson "immunized" the girl against the negative injunctions of her family and the laughter of schoolmates. Other "spontaneous" changes took place in the girl's family and social contexts as well. "They had no daughter to complain about at home. They had no one to laugh at at school. I did network therapy, didn't I?" he said.

Erickson worked predominantly from the inside outward (exteriorization) in helping individuals activate and develop the full range of psychological potentials that could help them act creatively on problems in living associated with self- and society-imposed limitations. His patients learned to cultivate the capabilities necessary to exteriorize new learnings and behave differently in family and social domains. Often by means of hypnosis, they learned to be less vulnerable to the destructive suggestions of others.

CONCLUSION

Both structural/strategic family therapies and Ericksonian hypnotherapy work indirectly in terms of their emphasis on clinically affecting patterns, not content, and on working metaphorically. Ericksonian hypnotherapy is a process that maximizes the exteriorization of interior events, it is a therapy spoken "indirectly" or in the unique private code of the individual client. The structural/strategic family therapy approaches emphasize interiorization of exterior events; working indirectly through interactional patterns, family therapists help people change their mental states.

Therapists realize that whether the approach is direct or indirect, interior changes are not automatically turned into exterior action. Some families and social institutions can overpower the best interior arrangements. Likewise, lethal symptoms may persist even after families have changed, representing a failure in spontaneous interiorization. Ultimately, practicing therapists hope to use these dialectically related approaches to arrive at a more systematic understanding of the point at which the individual unconscious converges with interpersonal processes. Theories and techniques that synchronize therapists' grasp of both inner and outer sources of a symptom are needed.

Haley (1963) and Laing (1972) made an analogy between the powers of the family over the individual and those of the hypnotists over a responsive subject. Haley compared the symptom—with its automatic component—to the automatic expression of trance behaviors. Montalvo (1976) showed specifically how a series of family interactions inadvertently culminated in multiperson amnesias for an event that had just occurred in a session; these "family amnesias" maintained a child's asthma. Over the past decade, many other clinicians around the world have routinely used hypnotic techniques to show how families and other less private social institutions "hypnotize" symptom bearers (Ritterman, 1980) and how symptom bearers entrance their families into perceiving them in handicapping ways.

In these days of the threat of nuclear war, when the influence of context over individual seems so vast and the suggestive power of the media so great, it is essential to understand (1) how family and society both directly and indirectly, organize the interior life of individuals without their conscious intention and (2) how people can mobilize their own resources, both inner and outer, to exercise their basic human right of personal freedom. Family therapists and Ericksonian hypnotherapists have much to offer each other in direct and indirect psychotherapeutic techniques and in other, broader understandings of the relationship between the elusive suggestive powers of individuals and those of social institutions within contemporary reality.

REFERENCES

Calof, D. (1985). Hypnosis in marital therapy: Toward a transgenerational approach. In J.K. Zeig (Ed.), *Ericksonian psychotherapy: II. Clinical applications* (pp. 71–91). New York: Brunner/Mazel.

Erickson, M. Personal Communication, 1976.

Erickson, M., & Rossi, E. *Hypnotherapy: An exploratory casebook.* New York: Irvington.

Erickson, M.H., & Rossi, E.L. (1979). The indirect forms of suggestion. In E.L. Rossi (Ed.), *The collected papers of Milton H. Erickson on hypnosis.* (Vol. 1). *The nature of hypnosis and suggestion* (pp. 452–477). New York: Irvington.

Green, R.J., & Freund, J.L. (Eds.). (1981). *Family therapy major contributions.* New York: International University Press.

Haley, J. (1963). *Strategies of psychotherapy.* New York: Grune & Stratton.

Haley, J. (1973). *Uncommon therapy: The psychiatric techniques of Milton H. Erickson.* New York: Norton.

Haley, J. (1980). *Leaving home.* New York: McGraw-Hill.

Haley, J. (1984). *Ordeal therapy.* San Francisco: Jossey-Bass.

Laing, R.D. (1972). *The politics of the family.* New York: Random House.

Lankton, S., & Lankton, C. (1983). *The answer within: A clinical framework of Ericksonian hypnotherapy.* New York: Brunner/Mazel.

Madanes, C. (1981). *Strategic family therapy.* San Francisco: Jossey-Bass.

Madanes, C. (1984). *Behind the one-way mirror: Advances in the practice of strategic therapy.* San Francisco: Jossey-Bass.

Minuchin, S. (1974). *Families and family therapy.* Cambridge, MA: Harvard University Press.

Minuchin, S., Rosman, B., & Baker, L. (1978). *Psychosomatic families.* Cambridge, MA: Harvard University Press.

Montalvo, B. (1976). Observations on two natural amnesias. *Family Process, 15,* 333–342.

Ritterman, M. (1980). Hypnostructural family therapy. In L. Wolberg & M. Aronson (Eds.), *Group and family therapy: An overview.* New York: Brunner/Mazel.

Ritterman, M. (1983). *Using hypnosis in family therapy.* San Francisco: Jossey-Bass.

Ritterman, M. (1985). Family context, symptom induction and therapeutic counterinduction: Breaking the spell of a dysfunctional rapport. In J.K. Zeig (Ed.), *Ericksonian psychotherapy: II. Clinical applications* (pp. 49–70). New York: Brunner/Mazel.

6

An Indirect Approach to Brief Therapy

Steve de Shazer, MS
Director
Brief Family Therapy Center
Milwaukee, Winsconsin

T RADITIONALLY, BRIEF THER-
apy focuses on problems and problem
solving (de Shazer, 1975; Weakland,
Fisch, Watzlawick, & Bodin, 1974),
rather than on the emotional or intrapsy-
chic aspects of problems. The prototype
for brief therapy has long been "symptom prescription." If a client complains
of feeling depressed, for example, the
therapist who has adopted this approach
has been likely to encourage the client to
become more depressed deliberately, resulting in the client actually feeling and
acting less depressed. An important
aspect of this approach involves determining the behaviors that have maintained the depressed feelings and,
minimally, helping the client to discon-
tinue these behaviors. The process of
"becoming more depressed" is built on
"reframing" the situation (i.e., describing the situation from a different point of
view) so that the task of becoming more
depressed, within the context of wanting
to be less depressed, makes sense to the
client. Similarly, fighting couples have
been told to fight more (but differently)
in order to end their fights. That is, brief
therapy was seen to focus directly on
stopping the client's complaint or problem.

This focus on interactional and/or in-
trapersonal problem solving has resulted
in greater and greater efforts to understand the nature of problems and ways to
solve them. Solutions have been examined only in relationship to the complaint
(de Shazer, 1982; Haley, 1976; Watzlawick, Weakland, & Fisch, 1974), on the
assumption that knowing the details and,

Note: The author wishes to thank his colleagues, Insoo Kim Berg, Eve Lipchik, Alex Molnar, Elam
Nunnally, Wallace Gingerich, Ron Kral, and Michele Weiner-Davis, for their contributions to the
development of the approach described in this presentation.

48

therefore, understanding the complaint or problem is necessary for resolution. However compelling this assumption may seem, recent work (de Shazer, 1985; de Shazer et al., 1986) suggests that the traditional way of looking at solutions may not be the most useful way.

A SOLUTION FOCUS

Solutions may be examined in relationship to goals. After all, the client's present and future satisfaction is of central importance in therapy. Simply, solutions can be seen to involve "a client doing something different to become more satisfied with his or her life." The sequence of events could be punctuated with the complaint as only an element in the client's past. The moment therapy is initiated by a call to set up an appointment, the current complaint is subject to redefinition; the solution begins in the present and continues into the future. This line of thought suggests that the nature of solutions (de Shazer, 1985) is of far greater interest than is the nature of complaints.

When describing an approach, stating some of the basic assumptions can make its nature and implications more evident. For instance, the complaints that clients present to therapists can be seen as involving a restricted set of behaviors, perceptions, thoughts, feelings, and expectations. Any exceptions to the complaint involve behaviors, perceptions, thoughts, feelings, and expectations that are outside the complaint's constraints. These exceptions and any other behaviors, perceptions, thoughts, feelings, and expectations *outside* the constraints of the complaint can be used

as building blocks in the construction of a solution. Within this framework, solutions are seen to involve both new behavior and increased satisfaction (different perceptions, thoughts, feelings, and expectations). Therefore, when solution focused, the therapist talks about changes, differences that make a difference, and solutions rather than talking about difficulties, complaints, and problems. As a rule of thumb, solutions involve determining what "works" so that the client can do more of it.

A young man started his first therapy session by stating that he had been depressed all his life. When asked how he knew he was "depressed" rather than "normal," he talked about the days when he did not feel depressed. On those days, his activities increased dramatically. He played basketball, golf, and tennis; he organized his activities with a systematic checklist. He saw none of these activities as anything more than proof that he was depressed (i.e., the exception proves the rule). He presented it this way: "I am depressed, and therefore I do not play golf, etc."

The therapist approached the client's problem from the opposite direction—the client did not play golf, etc. and, therefore, was depressed. Furthermore, the therapist saw the sports and organization by lists as "exceptions" to the rule that "I have been depressed all my life." Because playing tennis and organizing his activities helped the client to feel more "normal" and more satisfied with life, these activities could be used as building blocks to develop a solution.

A quick look at a map shows that there are many ways to get to Kansas City from Chicago by road, some quick and quite direct and some rather involved. The person in Chicago may choose any of the routes to Kansas City, including the interstate system, state highways, or some combination of these with county trunk roads and city streets; one route (solution) is not necessarily better than another. Interestingly, the routes from Chicago to Kansas City have very little to do with

- how the traveler reached Chicago in the first place
- what has kept the traveler from leaving Chicago earlier
- where in Chicago the traveler has been staying
- the nature of Chicago itself
- how long the traveler has been in Chicago

The fact that the traveler is in Chicago constrains only the number of options for sensible routes to Kansas City. Of course, the sensible route depends on what the traveler wants to see and who the traveler wants to visit on the way to Kansas City.

En route to Kansas City, there are many ways for the traveler to know that he or she is (1) no longer in Chicago and (2) on the right road; for example, the traveler may see signs "To Kansas City." These signs may provide satisfaction enough if a major part of the traveler's desire to go to Kansas City is simply a desire not to be in Chicago.

Most clients describe themselves as dissatisfied with their current situation, but they tend to be very unclear about their goals. They seem to be certain only that they want to be somewhere other than where they are now (the problematic situation—Chicago). When they have defined their goals (destination—Kansas City), various solutions (alternate routes to Kansas City) are open to them and the therapist. However, most clients do not know where they want to go. It would seem that this lack of specific goals would make brief therapy more difficult, except that the number of options (alternate routes) increases when the client wants only to be somewhere more satisfactory (no longer in Chicago). Solutions, therefore, can be described as more satisfactory situations (routes from Chicago) that can be reached by behaving differently (being in Muncie or Dayton or Kansas City).

In each case, there are exceptions. There are days when being in Chicago is not problematic or days when Chicago is a good place to be. Although these exceptions frequently seem insignificant, they are the raw material for solutions; they are clues to the kind of perceptual and behavioral changes that will resolve the problem. Simply seeing the situation differently may increase satisfaction; when seen from a different perspective (i.e., reframed), Chicago may be OK. Because of this shift in perception or construction of a new reality, the individual may behave differently while in Chicago, increasing his or her satisfaction there.

SAVING A MARRIAGE

In the early 1970s, a family sought therapy because, each morning at approximately 11:30, the 11-year-old daughter was reporting to the school nurse's office bent over with stomach pain. The nurse would call the mother, who would talk to the daughter, commiserate with her, and give her permission to lie down until the pain went away. Some days, the pain persisted; if the daughter was still in the nurse's office at 1 o'clock, the mother would go to school and pick up her daughter. The school administrators, the teachers, and the nurse became progressively more concerned as the parents' search for the cause of the stomach pain and its cure continued to be fruitless. An event that initially occurred once a month soon occurred once a week, then three times a week, but nothing seemed physically wrong.

During the first therapy session, the daughter described her stomach pains, the father described his back pains, and the mother and older daughter each described their frequent headaches. The parents were stoic about the pains, refusing to let the pains interfere with their lives and continuing to work. None of the pain seemed to have any physical cause, and there were days when each family member was pain-free.

The therapist prescribed a simple task: every night before the younger daughter's bedtime, each family member was to predict secretly whether each of the other three family members would have pains the next day. If possible, they were to list the criteria on which they based the prediction. In addition, each was to keep a record of days with pain and days without pain so that the predictions could be checked against the facts. This task might be seen as a "symptom prescription," since the pains were implicitly prescribed. Certainly nothing was said about stopping the pains. Of interest here, however, days without pain were also prescribed indirectly.

Over a month (a total of three sessions), the pain frequencies of all family members diminished, and the younger daughter was staying in school without apparent difficulty. On the way out of the office after the final session, the father said to the therapist, "Thanks for saving our marriage." The mother simply beamed.

At no time had either the husband or the wife mentioned any marital difficulties. The second and third sessions had been spent primarily on comparisons of predictions against facts and of what happened on days with pains against what happened on days without pains. The child's symptoms appeared unrelated to marital complaints; to the contrary, the marriage seemed both stable and satisfactory. Although the therapist did no deliberate indirect work on marital complaints, this experience demonstrates the usefulness and importance of indirect approaches.

Predicting someone else's pain, rather than (or in addition to) predicting personal pain, is an indirect approach. Instead of secretly dreading their own pain while wishing it would go way, each family member was asked to predict the others' pains; however, nothing was said about predicting their own pain. Even if the father was sure he was going to have pain the next day, there was some chance that the others might have predicted a pain-free day for him, causing him to doubt that he would have pain.

The solution to the unmentioned marital difficulties involved the family's different activity in the realm of the family members' pains, not in the marital interaction arena. Rather than stopping something, the therapy involved starting something that, in this case, seemed to have little or nothing to do with a major marital complaint—which was solved by accident. It is axiomatic that a change in one element of a system or in the relationship between elements leads to changes in other parts of the system. Therefore, provided that the change is relevant to the rest of the system, indirect approaches should be effective.

Improving a Marriage

When asked why he and his wife sought therapy, Mr. B. replied, "Sometimes our arguments lead to physical violence." This being enough of a statement of complaint to begin with, the therapist turned to Mrs. B., hoping to learn about any exceptions to that statement. The therapist asked her, "What happens when that doesn't?" Although taken aback, she started to describe the good periods between the fights. The ensuing discussion of what went right during the majority of their life together consumed most of the first therapy session. It became clear that their fights actually were few and far between, although the nature of these fights was indeed troublesome. Interestingly, each felt personally responsible for the violence and took credit for the efforts to prevent the violence without any awareness of the other's part. Throughout their 5 years together, they had tried many approaches, including therapy, to eliminate the physical violence between them. In fact, there had been some occasions on which together they had found ways to circumvent violence when they were arguing. Days before the first session, however, they had a physical altercation. Although they loved each other deeply, they had both come to question the wisdom of staying together.

In part to confirm that the nonviolent aspects of their relationship were legitimate building blocks for the solution to their complaint, the therapist asked, "Suppose that, one night while you were both asleep, there was a miracle and this problem was solved. Without talking about it, how would you know? What would he be doing differently? What would she be doing differently?" Their descriptions of the day after the "miracle" were remarkably like their descriptions of normal good days. Mr. B saw himself doing some new things, while Mrs. B. could see nothing new.

At the end of the first session, the therapist gave them the following message:

"I am impressed with how much you two obviously care about each other and how much effort you've put into solving the violence problem. Clearly, what works for you works well. But, after such a long time, the problem might have seemed unsolvable and, therefore, you might have—like a lot of couples—just split up. But you didn't, since you both know a good thing when you see it.

"A new business, a young child, all the travel—together and separately—all during the past 6 months are enough to stress and strain any relationship. But you two did not let that mess up the good stuff in your life. And that's impressive.

"With two such strong individuals, strong disagreements are inevitable—now and then—but, as you know, when such a relationship works, then creative solutions are possible.

"Between now and next time we meet, I would like each of you to pay attention to what the other one does that you want to see them continue to do."

At the end of the first session, the therapist knew little more about the complaint than had been revealed in Mr. B.'s opening statement. The session's entire focus had been on the behaviors that were effective for Mr. and Mrs. B. The therapist's task was to amplify these behaviors, not to stop the troublesome arguments that sometimes led to violence. The suggestions that they observe each other was based on the idea that "how he sees her seeing him" and "how she sees him seeing her" would influence the way that they saw themselves (Mead, 1934). Interactionally speaking, neither of them alone "caused" the violence. Therefore, if he sees her behaving differently toward him, he will see himself differently and may behave differently. She could be expected to respond similarly. Metaphorically, the intention was to change the shape of the doughnut in order to change the shape of the hole. By directly promoting the solution, the aim was to deal indirectly with the complaint.

When Mr. and Mrs. B. returned for the second session, they each reported several things that they wanted the other to continue doing. It was not until the end of the session was approaching that they reported a "nearmiss." They agreed that, in the past, a particular situation would probably have led to violence. This time, however, they saw themselves and each other do something different that stopped the violence. When she thought that the argument had reached a point at which he would normally withdraw, he gave her a hug instead. As he did not withdraw, she could not chase after him; therefore, she was forced to do something different also—tickle him. In fact, they reported an increased amount of hugging in both good moments and bad throughout the period following the nearmiss.

The therapist gave them this message at the end of the second session:

"I am impressed with what you've learned about each other and yourselves and about changing habits. I am struck by how open you are to each other's suggestions. I, of course, agree that life has its ups and downs and hope that you aren't shocked if you are unfortunate enough to have things again get out of hand.

"I am glad to see that you have found some new things that work and, therefore, hugging, tickling, funny faces, holding hands are the kind of thing you need to do more of; and anything else like that; you never know which creative new habits will work best."

Again, the focus of the session was on what behaviors were effective for Mr. and Mrs. B. Their spontaneous discussion of the "nearmiss" emphasized what they did that was new. Thus, the focus was on those aspects of their situations that could be useful in resolving the problem.

The third session (2 weeks later) and the fourth session (1 month after the third) continued the same theme. The primary question became "Just how confident do you two need to be that the violence is a thing of the past?" Using a scale with 10 as "no confidence" and 0 as "reasonable confidence," they rated their confidence level (in hindsight) as close to 10 prior to the first session. By the fifth session (1 month after the fourth session), he rated her at 1, while she rated him at 0. On the self-rating, both said 1.

This was the closing message to them:

> It seems that you two have things on the right track and are doing things to keep on the right track, things that work for each of you and your marriage. Now, several months ago, neither of you had confidence that you could do that, and neither of you knew that you knew how to do that. People are like that. There are lots of things we know that we don't know we know, and, therefore, we can surprise ourselves and each other.

Eighteen months later, things continue to go well in their marriage, and no arguments have led to violence.

The case of Mr. and Mrs. B. is typical of those in which (1) therapist and clients are able to develop a focus to their work and (2) there are exceptions to the complaint. If there are no significant exceptions, the first steps are aimed at developing exceptions or, at least, clear pictures of life after the problem has been solved (de Shazer, 1985). Regardless, the approach is indirect in the sense that the therapist and clients focus directly on promoting the solution rather than on resolving the complaint; the complaint is dealt with only indirectly within the context of developing a solution. When directly working on a solution, the therapist needs to know little about the complaint and the patterns that help maintain it.

In a sense, effective behaviors in one area of life, no matter how remote from the area of the complaint, can be used as metaphors for solutions in the complaint area. This type of metaphor readily "fits" clients, because it is derived from their own experience and, thus, is always clear to them. Furthermore, therapist-client cooperation is readily developed and promoted since the client is already doing exactly what the therapist is asking. At times, all that is required is that the client transfers effective behaviors from one area to another. At other times, simply increasing the frequency of the behaviors is enough.

CONCLUSION

Because clients and their therapists usually come from the same culture (both assuming a one-to-one relationship between complaint or problem and solution), it is sometimes useful for the therapist to elicit descriptions of the complaint area as a technique for

- promoting therapeutic rapport
- learning the clients' language, and
- meeting the clients' expectations

Clients expect to talk about complaints, and they will describe their complaints when they describe the differences between "what works" and "what doesn't work." The therapist's direct focus on solutions enables clients to talk indirectly about their complaints as they talk directly about solutions and potential solutions.

The techniques for constructing solutions to particular complaints are not necessarily connected to the nature of the complaints themselves (de Shazer, 1985). The relationship between complaint and solution appears to be rather indirect and, perhaps, tenuous. This suggests that the more traditional view of the direct complaint-solution relationship is simply a frame constructed by the participants. At least in part, the way in which individuals frame a situation produces their behaviors in that situation, and a solution-oriented frame increases the therapist's confidence in clients' ability to use what they know, but do not know that they know, to solve their problem.

REFERENCES

de Shazer, S. (1975). Brief therapy: Two's company. *Family Process, 14*(1), 78–93.

de Shazer, S. (1982). *Patterns of brief family therapy*. New York: Guilford Press.

de Shazer, S. (1985). *Keys to solution in brief therapy*. New York: Norton.

de Shazer, S., Berg, I.K., Lipchik, E., Nunnally, E., Molnar, A., Gingerich, W., & Weiner-Davis, M. (1986). Brief therapy: Focused solution development. *Family Process, 25*(2).

Haley, J. (1976). *Problem solving therapy*. San Francisco: Jossey-Bass.

Mead, G.H. (1934). *Mind, self and society*. Chicago: University of Chicago Press.

Watzlawick, P., Weakland, J., & Fisch, R. (1974). *Change: Principles of problem formation and problem resolution*. New York: Norton.

Weakland, J., Fisch, R., Watzlawick, P., & Bodin, A. (1974). Brief therapy: Focused problem resolution. *Family Process, 13*,141–168.

7

Indirect Therapy in the Schools

Ron Kral, MS
School Psychologist
School District of Elmbrook
Brookfield, Wisconsin
and
Research Associate
Brief Family Therapy Center
Milwaukee, Wisconsin

MENTAL HEALTH PROFESsionals in school settings routinely use direct approaches to treat students with behavior problems. This is reflected in the many articles on behavior modification, cognitive behavior modification, social skills training, Adlerian counseling, reality therapy, and teacher effectiveness training that are found in school psychology, school social work, and school counseling journals. These treatments are well-accepted in schools because they are consistent with a philosophy that values teaching people something new, much like teaching 6-year-olds to read. Skill training has its place and can be an effective way to treat school-related problems; however, indirect methods that make use of existing strengths and abilities can also be quite effective in bringing about behavioral changes in students.

In some cases, indirect therapeutic methods may be the treatment of choice for student problems. Some parents or teachers may not desire "training;" they just want to resolve the immediate problem in the simplest way possible, and doing something that they already know how to do or have done before seems simplest to them. Other adults, disturbed by the child's behavior, may be so exasperated with the situation that they lack the necessary motivation to learn a new technique. Finally, others may perceive no need for treatment, believing that the child simply should "get his act together" and "do as he's told." All these scenarios are similar in that the individual most able to make a change in the problem-maintaining pattern is unwilling or unable to learn and practice a new technique or approach.

If it is assumed that problem behavior is developed and maintained within the context of an interpersonal system, some element within that system must change before the disturbing behavior will change. For example, a teacher may reduce the frequency of a student's disruptive behavior (e.g., talking) by reframing that "misbehavior" as something useful or even desirable for the class (e.g., a signal that the teacher is moving too quickly for the class to follow). As suggested by the systemic hypothesis, most indirect therapeutic interventions in schools are directed at teachers, administrators, or parents, because the adults generally have a wider range of responses available to them, greater motivation to change, and more power in the situation than do typical students.

INDIRECT TECHNIQUES FOR SCHOOL-RELATED PROBLEMS

Within the context of the school, a variety of indirect techniques are available to intervene at the adult level, such as reframing, stories, "experiments," and positive blame. The purpose of these techniques is to facilitate a difference within the system, resulting in different behavior on the part of the student. Because these techniques change an individual's beliefs, behavior, or some combination of both, the adult responds to the student's problem behavior in a different way. The response is already in the behavioral repertoire of that adult, however; there is no need to "teach" new skills, only to combine old ones in new ways or to solve a "different" problem that the adult has solved before. These techniques are indirect as they focus on behaviors and/or beliefs other than those of the problem student.

Reframing

"I go over the possibilities and pick out a nice one," was the way Milton Erickson talked about reframing (Haley, 1985, p. 71). Changing the meaning of a behavior often changes the responses to the behavior. For example, a teacher who learns that a student's quiet, passive behavior is thoughtfulness rather than resistance is likely to be more patient with that student.

An assistant principal was told that a student's regular visits to the office were an indication of her growing trust in an adult, not an attempt to escape classes. Therefore, instead of disciplining the student for cutting class, which would lead to her suspension from school, the administrator scheduled "appointments" with her after school. The student remained in class, and the administrator began encouraging the student rather than labeling her a "troublemaker."

Stories

Therapists may use stories to widen the range of options available to a parent or teacher in dealing with a child. Often, an adult is encouraged to "do something different" the next time that the problem behavior occurs. This suggestion is followed by a story or two to illustrate the point.

A group of parents were discussing ways to get their children up for school in the morning. One mother complained about her daughter's resistance every morning. A second mother explained her approach. She had told her son that, since he was old enough to go to school, he was old enough for his own alarm clock. She took him to a store, and he picked out a clock for himself. His mother showed him how to use it, and he began to get up by himself, proud of his accomplishment. When the first mother tried the same tactic with her reluctant daughter, the results were equally good.

Experiments

An experiment is a task assigned to the teacher or parent. The purpose of the experiment is to establish some form of change in the pattern that exists around the problem behavior. De Shazer and Molnar (1984) provided prototypes of four useful tasks that can easily be adapted to the school setting. The tasks they described are:

- "Between now and the next time we meet, we (1) want you to observe, so that you can tell us (me) next time, what happens in your (life, marriage, family, or relationship) that you want to continue to have happen." (p. 298)
- "Do something different." (p. 300)
- "Pay attention to what you do when you overcome the temptation or urge to . . . (perform the symptom or some behavior associated with the complaint)." (p. 302)
- "A lot of people in your situation would have. . . ." (p. 302)

The authors described the specific problem patterns for which each of these tasks are appropriate. For example, asking teachers to "observe what a student does in class which the teacher would like to see continuing to happen" has proved to be a powerful intervention. This experiment not only minimizes the problem in the teacher's mind, but also provides valuable information about behaviors that can be encouraged to replace the problem behavior.

A teacher noted that the student paid attention when the instructor stood within 10 feet of him. She changed his seat and altered the pattern in which she walked around during class. These small changes eliminated his distractibility to the point that the teacher no longer considered it a problem.

Positive Blame

Nothing occurs *every* time. In fact, there are occasions when the problem behavior could have occurred, but did not. Once an exception to the "rule" has been identified, the teacher or parent is "blamed" for its occurrence. "What did you do differently those mornings when Monica got up and went to school?" Careful examination usually uncovers a difference in the adult's behavior. This difference can then be developed.

CASE EXAMPLE

All four indirect techniques can be combined in a single conference to change the behavior of a student indirectly.

Solved Already

Matt G. was a 12-year-old boy who had been enrolled in a class for emotionally disturbed children because of "depression" that interfered with his schoolwork. The reports suggested that his parents neither recognized nor responded to his depressive feelings. His father took a "pull yourself together" stance, while his mother tended to deny the existence of any problem in an overprotective, hovering manner. Both Mr. and Mrs. G. had initially resisted efforts to place Matt in a special class, but had finally agreed to this placement when Matt was in the sixth grade. Matt came to the attention of the child study team for further consideration as he entered the middle school. He began to have severe temper tantrums and refused to move from class to class. His problem behavior escalated to the point that he would lie on the floor outside the special class, yelling and refusing to go to gym class. Telephone calls to Mrs. G. were met with a sense of despair, as she was at a loss about what to do. In fact, she was beginning to resent the school staff's constant complaining.

In order to deal with this situation, a conference was planned. Mrs. G. routinely came to school meetings, but Mr. G. attended such meetings only rarely. The team, which included the school counselor, psychologist, social worker, assistant principal, and special education teacher, decided that, if both parents were not present, the conference would be postponed until they could come in together. The date was set.

At a preconference meeting of the team, each member was assigned a role. The teacher made an offhand comment at this meeting that, since the appointment had been made, Matt's behavior had improved

slightly. Following the "exception to the rule" idea described by de Shazer (1985), the team collected more information about these changes to be used at the conference.

Mr. and Mrs. G., appearing tense, came together for the meeting. According to plan, the teacher began the conference by listing Matt's inappropriate behaviors, a standard practice in almost every school conference. As the litany of Matt's "sins" continued, his parents were observed to be getting very angry. Before they could respond to the negatives, however, the social worker interjected, "What really confuses us is that Matt's behavior has begun to improve. What have you done to account for this?" [Positive blame.] Immediately, the tension in the room lifted.

Mr. and Mrs. G. appeared relieved, but confused. After carefully considering her response, Mrs. G. finally stated that she had not "forgiven" Matt for his last problem, which resulted in an after school detention. She had told him that she was angry because it had been necessary for her to leave work early to pick him up and that his misbehavior had better stop. She then refused to talk to him any further, something she had never done before. The psychologist complimented the parents for what they were doing. He stated that a review of earlier test data suggested that Matt was not depressed, but rather was "overwhelmed" by middle school and by life in general. He added that Mrs. G.'s approach appeared to be on the right track, because the structure provided when adults "take charge" firmly helps children who are overwhelmed. [Reframing.]

The focus of the meeting then shifted to the next step. Mr. and Mrs. G. were told several stories about other parents who had helped their children by remaining consistent in their expectations, but unpredictable in their response to misbehavior. The team shared with Mr. and Mrs. G. examples of approaches that had been effective, implying that these plans might not be exactly appropriate for Matt.

Mr. and Mrs. G. were then asked to determine in some unpredictable manner (e.g., a coin toss), which one of them would pick Matt up after his detentions in the future. They agreed willingly. Mrs. G. was happy that she would not always have to pick him up, and Mr. G. thought it would serve Matt right to wait an extra hour, until 5:00 when he finished work. [Experiment.]

Finally, Mr. and Mrs. G. were told that things would get worse before they would get better. Therefore, it would probably be necessary to meet with the psychologist in a week or two to decide what to do next. The counselor added that the psychologist always had useful ideas, but that most of them were very unusual and strange.

Matt's behavior continued to improve after the conference. Mr. and Mrs. G. requested one follow-up meeting with the psychologist. They did not ask for new ideas, however, but rather wanted some input about their "spontaneous" efforts. Mr. G.

had calmly discussed his fears about Matt's future with them and had suggested to Matt that he would quite possibly end up in jail as a result of his tantrums. Therefore, Mr. G. had tried to arrange a visit to a jail so that Matt could see what it was like. He was unable to do this, so he had decided to transform Matt's room into a cell. Mr. and Mrs. G. had taken everything but his clothes and bed out of Matt's room and stored all his belongings in the basement. After this, they noticed a marked change in his behavior. He was generally more compliant and even began eating his meals with the family, something that he had not done for several years. The meeting with the psychologist revolved around the appropriate time to put things back in the room as Matt's behavior continued to improve. A contact several months later with both the teacher and the parents indicated that Matt was progressing in both settings.

During the conference on Matt's problems, a "shotgun" approach was used (i.e., several techniques were used simultaneously). Work was also done on several levels in that the social worker, the psychologist, and the counselor had acted as a "subcommittee" in dealing with the administration and teaching staff, reframing Matt's behavior for them, and offering direct strategies, such as after school detentions. In addition, they fostered a positive working relationship between home and school by reframing Mr. and Mrs. G. as interested and capable parents who simply needed some new "tricks" for dealing with Matt. Although no contacts were made with Matt, his behavior changed as a result of changes in the system.

Mr. and Mrs. G. were not trained, nor were they told precisely what to do about Matt's behavior. Instead, they were empowered to *continue* changing his behavior by being "blamed" for a difference that had already become apparent. This follows de Shazer's concept of the exception to the rule (1985); in this case, the rule was that his parents had been able to obtain Matt's compliance even when it came to eating dinner with the family. The parents' empowerment was strengthened as Matt's behavior was reframed as the result of being overwhelmed rather than of being depressive. Parents can help children who are overwhelmed; only trained therapists can deal with depression.

After his parents' potential influence over Matt's behavior had been discovered, further possibilities were opened up within the parents' own unique style through the use of stories. Other parents had successfully dealt with equally troubling situations by being creative, and so could they. If they could not, the psychologist would be happy to prescribe something strange. Their response was to develop their own plan as if to avoid doing whatever weird thing the psychologist had in mind.

Finally, Mr. and Mrs. G. were asked to conduct a little experiment designed to underscore the message that they were in charge—not Matt. Their response to the intervention was to take charge in an even more significant fashion, which produced the desired result. The intervention did not "teach" Mr. and Mrs. G. new skills in the usual sense, nor did it require them to learn a new vocabulary unique to some theoretical

model. Instead, they were encouraged to "do something different" based on new information (i.e., the blame and the reframe), while the realm of possible new behaviors was expanded by the stories and the experiment.

Getting Older Now

While parents generally have more power than teachers have over a student's life, the techniques that are effective with parents are also effective with teachers.

The school psychologist was approached by a high school teacher who worked with emotionally disturbed students. She was concerned about Tom, a 17-year-old boy who had a generally pleasant nature, but was failing classes. Tom was adopted, and his teacher felt that this was at the core of his problem. Tom did not get along well with his parents, and they had essentially given up trying to solve his school problems. Ms. D., the teacher, had spent a great deal of time talking with Tom about his schoolwork and his problems with his parents, but she had not made any noticeable changes. She hoped that the psychologist would help Tom resolve the adoption issue, therefore "freeing him up" to succeed in school. The psychologist discussed the possibility of therapy with Ms. D. and asked that, before he attempted to engage Tom in therapy, she help determine the extent to which the adoption issue played a role. She agreed.

The psychologist went on to suggest that, in many ways, Tom's behavior was normal for a 17-year-old. He was in the process of separating from his parents and experimenting with independence by "doing his own thing" at school. [Reframe.] If this were the case, he would most likely respond to an experiment that took advantage of his need to be himself. Ms. D. was instructed to stop trying to "help" Tom as she had in the past. Rather, she was to apologize to him for not trusting his ability to take care of himself. In fact, she was to go even further and suggest that he find a job so that he could move into his own place when he became 18 and even drop out of school at that time if he wished. Initially, Ms. D. was reluctant to consider this approach, but she agreed when the psychologist pointed out that this was only an experiment. She could return to helping him after she had given this a trial.

At first, Tom appeared to agree with Ms. D.'s suggestions. After a week, however, he began to protest a bit and told her that it might be a good idea to graduate from high school. During the second week, he came to school with a new backpack and started to carry all his books to class, something he had never done in the past. Noticing this small change, Ms. D. became even more forceful in her stance. She began to talk about the value of a high school equivalency degree and said that "maybe" Tom could pass those tests. He was not interested, particularly since he had been unable to find a job.

Ms. D. consulted the psychologist again. She did not mention the adoption issue. She asked if the psychologist would wait before seeing Tom individually, because he was now doing some work in several of his classes. During this meeting, she said that, whenever Tom seemed to be slipping back into his old behavior pattern, she again brought up the subject of dropping out or moving away from home. Tom usually responded negatively to her remarks and subsequently seemed to apply himself a bit more. When he worked, she assisted him if he asked, but she never went out of her way to help or nag as she had done in the past. After a semester of this approach, Tom had failed only one course, which was a notable improvement for him. He openly expressed a desire to graduate, even though it would be necessary for him to stay in school an extra year. In addition, Ms. D. reported that she now understood that Tom was old enough to face the reality of his situation.

In this case, the power of reframing was used to change a teacher's perception of a student. Ms. D. accepted the "new possibility" enough to attempt an experiment with Tom. The experiment was intended to shift her behavior from helping, which had proved ineffective, to challenging Tom. No one had challenged Tom before, because he had been considered "too damaged emotionally" to take care of himself. In the end, he continued to need help with schoolwork because of some underlying learning problems; the help now came as he wanted it, however. He appeared to be responding to the frame that he was "normal" and could take care of himself.

CONCLUSION

School-related problems can be effectively treated with indirect therapy techniques. Teachers, administrators, and parents already possess the necessary skills to resolve the difficulties that face them in dealing with student problems. Certainly, the same or similar approaches could be used with individual students. For the most part, however, the adults are more motivated and able to change. Therefore, in the interest of efficiency, treatment efforts should start with them.

REFERENCES

de Shazer, S. (1985). *Keys to solution in brief therapy*. New York: Norton.

de Shazer, S., & Molnar, A. (1984). Four useful interventions in brief family therapy. *Journal of Marital and Family Therapy, 10*(3), 297–304.

Haley, J. (Ed.). (1985). *Conversations with Milton H. Erickson, M.D.* (Vol. 3). *Changing children and families*. New York: Triangle Press.

8

The Uses of Humour in Therapy

Brian Cade, BA, CSW
Sydney, Australia

Humour . . . the ability to see three sides of one coin.

Ned Rorem

The best thing about humour is that it shows people that they're not alone.

Sid Caesar

Our lives, I propose, extend between the poles of tragedy and comedy, but we possess more freedom than we realize to experience our circumstances and ourselves in tragic or comic guise.

Harvey Mindess

If we recognize what is atrocious and laugh at it, we can master the atrocious.

Eugene Ionesco

THE WRITER ROBERT BENCHley once commented that "defining and analysing humour is a pastime of humourless people." It seems to be impossible to teach people to be funny, and an understanding of the mechanics of humour does not help very much in the invention of jokes. Therapists with a sense of humour can be encouraged to widen their therapeutic repertoires to include this facet of themselves, however, a facet that their professional training may have undervalued or even proscribed. Bateson once commented, "It is very strange that I never get any encouragement from psychiatric audiences when I want to talk about art or humour. I sometimes think there must be some sort of lack—I mean a gap—in the professional soul" (quoted in Berger, 1978).

Humour, according to Kane, Suls, and Tedeschi (1977), "is essentially a social psychological phenomenon and not merely a biological release or a cognitive process" (p. 13). It evolves as part of a relationship between a source and a recipient. It needs spontaneity for its creation and a degree of receptivity for its effects, neither of which can easily be mandated. Following the publication of an earlier article (Cade, 1982) on the creative potentials of humour in the work of a therapeutic team, for example, groups of visitors to our clinic would sit eagerly waiting for the flow of jokes to begin; however, we found ourselves becoming more and more serious, trapped in a classic "be spontaneous!" bind with not a funny idea in our heads. The more we tried to think of something funny, the more serious we seemed to become.

Therapists need feel no obligation to "be funny!" but should be open to the possibilities of using any amusing, absurd ideas that occur spontaneously during the process of therapy. The effectiveness of humour for facilitating the development of a relationship, for putting people at their ease, for de-fusing tension, and for creating a distance between a person and the source of his or her distress is well recognised by most therapists. Humour is most therapeutic when it is *inclusive*, most harmful when it is *exclusive*. Therefore, understanding, empathy, and positive regard for the process of therapy are important. As Farrelly and Brandsma observed (1974), even sarcasm, usually a more aggressive, belittling, excluding form of humour, can be used by a therapist as long as it is "qualified by his facial expression, tone of voice, etc." (p. 109). When a therapist is struggling either consciously or unconsciously with negative responses to a family or family member, such as anger or fear, humour is more likely to be perceived as disrespectful, belittling, uncaring, aggressive, and exclusive. As Levant (1984) commented in talking of Carl Whitaker's use of the absurd, "It must be done in a caring,

loving way; and, contrary to the usual practice of paradoxical techniques, it is best done without rational thought or plan, but rather intuitively, even unconsciously" (p. 173).

HUMOUR AND CREATIVITY

Koestler (1975) believed that the creative force in humour, like the creative force in art and science, arose from the discovery of previously hidden connections, from the juxtaposition and subsequent integration of seemingly unrelated spheres of discourse. He asserted that

> the creative act, in so far as it depends on unconscious resources, presupposes a relaxing of the controls and a regression to modes of ideation which are indifferent to the rules of verbal logic, unperturbed by contradiction, untouched by the dogmas and taboos of so-called common sense. (p. 178)

For its expression, humour needs two frames of reference: (1) the normal, the expected, set against and restrained by the recipient's usual definitions of reality; and (2) the intrusion of the previously unrelated, the unexpected and unpredictable, and the absurd, unrestrained by normal definitions of reality. From the juxtaposition of these two frames of reference arises a suspension of the rules of "reality." During this brief suspension of reality, creativity is unlocked, and leads to new insights, new perspectives, and liberation from the constraints of learned "mental sets."

Erickson and Rossi (1976) have asserted that the therapeutic potential of humour lies in the "mechanism of activating unconscious association patterns and response tendencies that suddenly summate to present consciousness with an apparently 'new' datum or behavioral response'' (p. 226). At any point in their lives, individuals' belief frameworks dictate what aspects of experience they select as *figure* against the *ground* of all other possible selections, as well as how they interpret and respond. Humour, with its potential disruption of the normal figure-ground relationships, can introduce a greater fluidity of selection and, thus, of interpretation and response. As Levine observed (1977),

> By the adoption of the humerous attitude we have the license to do outrageous things and think outrageous thoughts. To be ''in humour'' gives us freedom from rational and moral inhibitions, and for the moment we have the license to say and act without regard for logic, proper conduct, and even offensiveness. The degrees of freedom are set only by the social context. We can act and talk silly, poke fun at the mighty, be profane, and play at sex. (p. 135)

A couple sought marital therapy, obviously at the wife's instigation. For half an hour she heatedly elaborated on all her husband's faults, while he sat calmly, showing little interest in the proceedings. When asked his opinion, he declared that he did not know why his wife went on and on so, adding "Between you and me, I think she needs to see a psychiatrist."

I found it extremely difficult to interrupt the woman's flow of talk. She either talked over the top of what I was trying to say or ignored my comments or questions. An extremely successful businessman and local politician, the husband refused to be drawn into a discussion of any of the issues raised, commenting at one point that he was bored, saying that he was a busy man, and asking how long the session would be. I noticed, however, that the woman constantly

"pulled her punches," either by smiling in a way that tended to disqualify the vehemence apparent in her voice or by verbally putting herself down in relation to her husband, denying the seriousness of her complaints.

Eventually, I interrupted and asked the woman in a very serious tone of voice, "Have you thought of shooting him?" The woman carried on talking for several seconds, then stopped in midsentence, turned, and asked me to repeat what I had said. I again made my suggestion. She laughed and asked me if I was really serious. "Yes, I certainly am. From how you have described your husband, if you are right in what you say, I'm surprised you have not thought of it yourself."

The husband immediately began to show an interest in the proceedings. Both of them listened attentively as I elaborated, solemnly, on some other methods she might use to do away with her husband, such as mixing ground glass or rat poison into his dinner, or pushing him under a bus or down the stairs. I acknowledged that, of course, she would undoubtedly end up in prison, but it would be a small sacrifice compared to the satisfaction that she would gain from finally fixing him for all that he had done to her over the years of their marriage. They looked at each other in silence for a few moments and then both burst out laughing, turning to me to find out what else I had to say.

Using humour, I recognized (and expressed) the anger that she was feeling, the ''punch'' she had been ''pulling.'' I had taken it seriously, albeit through a joke. Both partners began also to take it seriously and became equally involved in the therapy, which began to move in a more productive direction.

INCLUSIVE VS. EXCLUSIVE HUMOUR

Inclusive humour joins the participants in an alliance in which all parties laugh together at the absurdity of an idea, event, or attitude. In therapy, the butts of the humour are usually the problematic behaviours, beliefs, or attitudes adjudged to be maintaining symptoms, not the patient or patients themselves. Patients are invited or encouraged, either verbally or nonverbally, to join in the joke and, thus, to take a more distant and new view of their problems.

In contrast, exclusive humour makes one of the participants or a group the butt of the joke. The recipient or recipients do not, nor are they invited to, share in the humour. Although exclusive humour may at times be used as a challenge to provoke a change, it is not usually therapeutic and is more likely to be experienced as a personal attack by the recipient or recipients.

In the case just described, for example, the husband could easily have experienced my advice to his wife as an attack upon him, an expression of an alliance with her, in the face of which he might have become more resistant to therapy. Alternatively, the wife could have experienced my advice as sarcasm, an expression of a coalition with him, and felt belittled. It was imortant for me to be in a neutral position, seeing neither as more "to blame," so that both could feel included in the humour and could laugh *with* me at themselves (and

through the laughter begin to approach the anger in their relationship). It is clearly essential for therapists to maintain a nonjudgmental attitude.

It is arguably impossible for therapists, over any extended period of time, to disguise our basic diagnosis; it will inevitably be betrayed, albeit at an unconscious level, via the many non-verbal behaviours through which information can be exchanged. This is especially true where we hold a strongly negative or blaming view of a particular individual or group. (Cade, 1985, p. 44)

HUMOUR IN LANGUAGE OR ACTION

Madanes (1984) differentiated between two broad approaches to the use of humour in therapy. "One is based primarily on the use of language to redefine situations. The other relies on organizing actions that change a course of events and modify sequences of interaction" (p. 116). Language is used to reframe or relabel events, giving behaviours, ideas, and attitudes a new and potentially more flexible meaning. Madanes compared the use of actions to slapstick. Individuals, couples, or families are encouraged to behave in seemingly incongruous, exaggerated, or unexpected ways, either in the therapy sessions or as a between-sessions assignment, in order to interrupt a repetitive sequence. The therapist may also be involved in such a slapstick routine.

Madanes commented also on the importance of laughing *with* rather than *at* a patient. She noted that it is important for the therapist to have "the ability to tolerate ridicule, to appear absurd, to risk loss of face." She went on to propose that "what makes change possible is the therapist's ability to be optimistic and to see what is funny or appealing in a grim situation. Humour involves the ability to think at multiple levels and in this way is similar to metaphorical communication'' (p. 137).

A family was brought to me by a social worker who had asked for an urgent consultation. He felt stymied and was concerned that the identified patient, a 13-year-old boy, was "on the slippery slope." The family consisted of a twice-divorced, single woman of 33, and three children: James, aged 16; Terry, the 13-year-old patient; and Carol, aged 12.

Terry looked disinterested as the social worker began to outline the problems that had resulted in trouble with the police and had brought him to the attention of several social agencies. He had been assessed by a child psychiatrist, a paediatrician, and had had two periods of residential treatment. I turned to the boy and commented, "So you collect social workers, do you? Have you ever thought of trying stamps instead?" Terry grinned and began to show some interest in what was being said.

The social worker described how he had become increasingly concerned at the boy's poor response to the various attempts to help him. Recently, Terry had begun to sniff glue, and he seemed to be getting progressively more difficult to handle.

"Do you mean he's becoming a hopeless case?" I asked.

"Well," the worker replied, "one doesn't like to think in those terms, but that more or less sums it up."

"Yes," I commented, "but if your hobby is collecting social workers, then the best way of doing that is to be a hopeless case." I turned to Terry. "You collect lots of them that way, don't you?" Terry grinned and nodded knowingly.

"Have you ever thought of putting them all in a book? You could call it *Social Workers I Have Known*—you could publish it later on." Terry laughed out loud.

As the session progressed, it became obvious that Terry was very much connected to his mother and worried about her isolation. Since her second husband had deserted her 6 years earlier, she had had no men friends.

"What's wrong with the men in your area?" I asked.

"There's nothing wrong with them," he replied. "It's that she'll never go out. She hasn't been to the pub in years. She only goes down to the shops, and then only if one of us will go with her."

"If you were one of the local men, would you ask to take her for a drink?"

"Yes." Terry smiled proudly at his mother, who was following this conversation with considerable interest.

"But I suppose you're too young to take her into a pub, at present," I mused, sadly.

We went on to explore his mother's fear of trusting another man. She joined in the discussion, declaring herself to be "fat and unapproachable." Her opinion of herself was low, and she did not think that she would ever meet a man whom she would be able to trust. Then, laughing, she commented that Terry had once said that he would stay to look after her in her old age.

"Do you think she needs a husband?" I asked Terry.

Terry nodded.

"Will she accept you?"

He grinned.

At the end of the session, the social worker suddenly announced to me that he would soon be leaving for another job. I turned to Terry. "So you may have to find your mother another one." He nodded, sadly. His mother complained of the constant need to get to know new workers. I asked Terry, "Until Mum can trust herself to find another man who will be more constant to her, if she ever trusts herself, does this mean you've got to keep finding her social workers? Until you're old enough to marry her yourself that is."

Terry gave a wry smile. His mother immediately began to question the worker about whether it was absolutely necessary for his agency to send another social worker. Simultaneously, I was confiding in Terry that social workers make good husbands, because no one can get close enough to them to be too hurt when they leave.

Two months later, Terry's behaviour had improved dramatically. His mother looked much brighter and insisted that things were so much improved that they definitely did not need another worker on their case.

The gentle humour in this session not only intrigued and engaged this therapy-wise family, but also introduced a new framing for Terry's behaviour, touching on his concern about his mother and on

what, in other frameworks, might be seen as an Oedipal mother-son relationship. This session also stood in dramatic contrast to the heavy, increasingly pessimistic nature of the family's recent therapy experiences. At no point did we discuss these issues ''seriously'' as a part of the problem.

A 30-year-old woman rang to arrange an urgent appointment. She had recently been jilted by an older man, her ex-employer, with whom she had been having an affair for some 4 years. He was planning to marry someone else, and she had become obsessed with trying to win him back, sending him many letters and flowers, contriving to meet him, driving past his house and his place of work, walking up and down outside his house. She had had several confrontations with her "rival," and the man had become increasingly abusive over the last few weeks, finally arranging for his lawyer to send her a letter that warned her to leave him alone lest legal action be taken.

She could not stop thinking of him and had continued trying to contact him, however. She was, by now, petrified at the thought of being summonsed to appear in court. She would not be able to bear the shame or to forgive herself for the distress it would cause her aged mother, with whom she still lived. She recognized that, all through the relationship, he had treated her badly. "I know he had other women, lots of them, and only came round when he had no one else to have sex with. But I want him to know how much he has hurt me."

I told her that some therapists would advise her to try to forget this man, to respect herself and not to sell herself so cheaply, to resist the urge to throw herself after this man who did not deserve such loyalty. I, however, could well understand her need to be absolutely sure that she could not win him back. My criticism was not that she was trying to win him back, but that she was not being creative enough.

I advised her to curtail all other activities and concentrate totally on this important task. She was not to worry about making a fool of herself. The world would eventually understand. Others might define her behaviour as that of a lovelorn adolescent, but I respected her need to be sure that he was gone for good.

I suggested that she try chaining herself to the railings outside his house or laying down in front of his car as he tried to leave for work and again in the evening as he tried to leave for home. She could make her face pale with stage makeup (she had been a member of an amateur drama group) and sing songs of unrequited love outside his house. She could hire a group of musicians to serenade him outside his bedroom window, a ploy that might be most effective when he was "entertaining" his new woman. She could write poems and recite them from the roadway through a public address system (I knew a place where she could hire one).

The woman began to laugh. "You're not taking me seriously, are you?" I protested that, on the contrary, I was taking her problem extremely seriously. Why should he get away with treating her in such a cavalier fashion? He should be forced to know exactly how she felt. Had she thought of taking a scrubbing brush and cleaning the steps and the path leading up to the door of his house, perhaps even the road outside his gate, so that he should not soil his shoes? She began to giggle.

I saw her infrequently. She rejoined the drama group, beginning to take up her life again. Every now and then she would have the urge to contact him, but would contact me instead to ask my advice. I would advise dramatic gestures, such as those outlined earlier. She would laugh. One time she brought a letter that she had recently composed to ask me whether she should send it. I said that she certainly should, but suggested several embellishments. She tore the letter up and threw it away, laughing that she should have been so silly even to have considered sending it.

In this case, I took the woman's position and exaggerated it, turning the therapy into a kind of pantomime in which I suggested increasingly ridiculous approaches to her problem. She would laugh at the absurdity of the ideas and begin to engender counterarguments to them, thus reversing the usual process of therapy. It was not intended that the woman carry out the suggestions made; in the following case, however, a family was intended to carry out the pantomime offered.

A family sought therapy because of concern about the 15-year-old daughter, Sally. She was constantly fighting with her parents, who saw her as stubborn and deceitful. They also feared that she was becoming promiscuous. The parents seemed to have little in common, with many covert issues between them, and they disagreed about how the children should be handled. They had three other children: Joanne, aged 14, whom they described as "a treasure, who helps in the house, never gives us any worries, and is doing extremely well at school"; and identical twins, Fiona and Sian, aged 12.

The father, a prison officer, had very clear and strict ideas about running the family. Whenever problems occurred he would convene family meetings "to get to the bottom of things." These meetings seemed to consist primarily of accusations and counteraccusations, the elaboration of lists of "crimes," and the presentation of "evidence" either for or against the "accused." The therapist was being invited, as it were, to act as judge.

The main battles were between Sally and her parents; Joanne would attempt to be fair to both sides, and the twins would basically just watch, sometimes with anxiety, sometimes with giggles. Although the parents presented themselves as in agreement, it seemed to me that, in her battles with each parent, Sally was in some ways acting as a "hit woman" for the other. In spite of the tensions, however, the family also demonstrated a capacity for play.

At the end of the first session, the family seemed well engaged with the therapist and motivated to try anything that was suggested. They were instructed that, although they could ignore the normal parent-child differences of opinion that happen in all families, the twins were to call a halt to any serious argument between Sally and one of the parents and immediately to convene a family court hearing. Neither Sally nor the parent in question was to put his or her own case, nor could they communicate directly with each other. Joanne was to become advocate for the aggrieved parent, and the other parent was to become advocate for Sally. The protagonists could brief their representatives, however, presenting evidence where available, examining witnesses, and identifying any mitigating circumstances. The case was to be heard by the twins, who would act as a two-person jury. They were not to make any judgments, only to note the evidence and be prepared to offer their verdict to the therapist during the next session. With much laughter, the family agreed to this.

When they returned 2 weeks later, all agreed that the atmosphere in the house was vastly improved. Their one attempt at a "court hearing" had reduced them all to fits of laughter. They had called that particular hearing over a rather trivial issue "just to see what it would be like." In fact, there had been no major arguments. Sally had become more involved with the family and was no longer behaving in the provocative way that had previously been upsetting her parents. Although there were still issues to be worked on in the therapy, particularly between the parents, the problems presented at the beginning did not reappear.

"PLAY-FRAMES" AND SURPRISES

Fry (1963) differentiated between humour that is accompanied from the start by cues that denote a "play-frame" around the episode and humour that is not prefaced by such cues, in which the element of surprise is an important ingredient. In discussing play-frames, Fry commented:

> Usually these frames are established at the beginning of the humourous episode. A wink, a smile, a gurgle in the voice will set the stage before the joke begins its evolution. The Joker may communicate the message by the posture of his body or an *almost* un-noticed movement of his arm. His nose may wiggle; he may emphasize various sounds or frequencies in his voice. (p. 141)

Sometimes the play-frame is introduced directly by statements such as "Let me tell you a funny story." or "Have you heard the one about?" When inviting people spontaneously to try something different, I often use as a story a case reported by de Shazer (1985). The story concerns the parents of an 8-year-old boy who was throwing frequent temper tantrums. They had tried everything and were at the end of their tether.

> At the end of the session with just the parents, the therapist told them to, "Do something different next time Josh throws a tantrum, no matter how strange, or weird, or off-the-wall what you do might seem. The only important thing is that whatever you decide to do, you need to do something different." During the next tantrum father gave Josh a cookie without saying a single word. The tantrum stopped. When mother next witnessed a tantrum, she danced circles around the boy while he kicked and screamed. The tantrum stopped. Subsequently,

neither the parents nor the school reported any tantrums. (p. 126)

I usually conclude the story by saying, "Now, what therapist would have thought of such solutions? Even if a therapist had advised such actions, most parents would be hard to convince that they would work and would probably, if they had been persuaded to try, have applied them without conviction and self-consciously rather than spontaneously." Most people find this story amusing, and a number have gone on to make changes in their lives, referring back to the story in subsequent sessions.

When no prior cues are given to define the situation as humourous, the humourous statement or event comes as a total surprise to the recipient who, only at the end, is able to appreciate the joke (or not).

A woman, after 20 years of psychiatric treatment, was struggling to stop taking tranquilizers and to start making something of her life. She was suffering from frequent panic attacks and claimed to be unable to swallow any food unless she had consumed several glasses of whisky to relax her throat muscles. Only then could she eat anything, and the food needed to be well mashed. In fact, she had recently bought a food blender and was making mushy soups with it.

She seemed determined to finish with the drugs and, during the second session, showed me a diary with ticks against the days that she had survived without the "help" of any medication. I asked her how she was going to reward herself when she reached 24 ticks in her diary. This thought intrigued her, and she began to muse about how nice it would be to go to a restaurant and enjoy a full three-course meal without having to drown herself in alcohol. "But, of course," she said sadly, "there'll be no chance of that. I'd end up gagging and choking and making a complete fool of myself."

I asked her what she would like to order if she were able to go ahead with such a treat. She considered a range of starters and eventually decided on a prawn cocktail. For the main course, she said she would love to eat a medium rare steak with boiled potatoes and broccoli. To complete the meal, she would have coffee with cheese and cracker biscuits. I asked her whether she knew of a restaurant where she could order such a meal. She replied that there was a very pleasant little restaurant quite near where she lived. It had a number of single tables where a woman on her own would not be too conspicuous. I asked what the staff were like; were they helpful? She confirmed that they were.

"So you will be able to ask, without too much embarrassment, for a table against the wall next to a power point?"

She looked puzzled for a few moments, then burst out laughing. "You mean to plug the blender in?"

"Yes. The prawn cocktail would liquidise easily. And I'm sure the staff would not mind if you popped briefly into the kitchen to rinse the blender out before the next course. You'd have to chop the steak up into small pieces, but the potatoes and broccoli should present you with no difficulties. I am unsure, however, about the cracker biscuits and the cheese. They might turn into a bit of a mess."

The woman was vastly amused at the idea and continued to giggle throughout the rest of the session. I did not return to the idea of a meal, but finished the interview by reiterating that she ought to find a way to reward herself when she achieved 24 ticks in her diary.

A week or so later, the woman booked into a hotel in a small country town. That night, she treated herself, without any prior drinks, to a three-course meal; the main course was a steak with French fried potatoes. She had no trouble swallowing. Although this was by no means the end of her problems, it was her first major breakthrough and her first real sense that her problems could be surmounted.

At no point during the earlier stages of this episode was this woman given any cue that I was slowly building up to a joke. As she conjoured up the meal in her mind, temporarily suspending the "reality" of her condition, the woman looked both sad and wistful. The sudden introduction of the absurd notion that she should take her food blender to the restaurant probably came when she was about to reimpose the "reality" of her situation and argue the impossibility of going through with such a treat. Maybe the joke blocked the total reimposition of that "reality," diverted her attention away from it, and allowed the wistfulness to continue until it became a determination to try.

THE PROVOCATIVE USES OF HUMOUR

Farrelly and Brandsma (1974) listed seven types of humour that can be used provocatively to elicit new responses from patients:

1. exaggeration—the overstatement or understatement of aspects of belief, affect, behaviour, relationships, or goals
2. mimicry—role play of aspects of affective responses, beliefs, and behaviours
3. ridicule—mockery not only of the patient's ideas or behaviours, but also of the therapist's role and "professional dignity"
4. distortion—deliberate misunderstanding and misinterpretation of communications
5. sarcasm—cutting, hostile, contemptuous, or caustic remarks
6. irony—(a) Socratic irony, in which a pretence of ignorance is assumed; (b) dramatic irony, in which the incongruities between desired outcomes and probable outcomes are highlighted
7. jokes—the use of incongruity and of the figure-ground reversals that occur in punch lines

Farrelly and Brandsma continually underlined the importance of using all types of humour within a therapeutic relationship in which warmth and positive regard are continually demonstrated, usually through posture, facial expression, and tone of voice. In the security of such a relationship, even the occasional use of sarcasm can provide a therapeutic challenge, although this type of humour is only rarely appropriate. It must be remembered that it is not the *person* who is the butt of the humour, but his or her ideation, attitudes, beliefs, behaviours,

or affective responses; the song, not the singer.

Some of the types of humour identified by Farrelly and Brandsma (1974) have been demonstrated in earlier case examples. An amusing example of distortion occurred in an interview conducted by Professor Mara Selvini-Palazzoli and Dr. Luigi Boscolo. The identified patient was a promiscuous young woman whose father had just been telling the therapists the extent to which she was a problem to the family. Asked how long these difficulties had been occurring, the father declared that she had been a problem since the age of 2. With a shocked expression and an incredulous tone of voice, Professor Selvini-Palazzoli asked, "She's been promiscuous since she was 2?"

A family consisting of middle-aged parents and a withdrawn, "borderline psychotic" son were giving little information away. It was obvious that the mother and the son were very involved with each other. The father, a mathematician who seemed to be inhabiting a totally private universe, was treated by his wife with a mixture of indulgence and exasperation. Throughout the session, when talking to the woman, I deliberately and consistently mixed up the names, using the boy's name when referring to "your husband" and the husband's name when talking about "your son." After a while, the woman began to correct me. I mused about the reasons that I could not get the names right. Eventually, the woman commiserated with me, admitting wryly that it must be rather difficult in that her husband was just like a big, irresponsible child. She received, she said, more emotional support from her son than she received from her husband.

Farrelly and Brandsma (1974) demonstrated the use of sarcasm in describing the case of a promiscuous woman who tells her therapist that she has finally secured a job that pays well. The therapist responds to this news suspiciously and in a sarcastic tone of voice, says, "Oh yeah, how did you persuade him to hire you, Sweetheart?" Blushing, the patient replies, "It *wasn't* like that!" (1974, p. 110)

Irony proved useful in the case of a depressed woman who still felt enormously guilty about many things in her past and current relationships. I agreed with her that she should take *some* responsibility for these things, but expressed surprise that she was so ready to take *all* the responsibility. I pointed out that this was a potentially very useful talent, however. There was an important role that she could play for other people. Like Jesus, she could relieve them of their guilt. In many ways she was like a "blame sponge," soaking up any guilt that was around. I began to offer her some of my guilts to carry for me. For example, I sometimes felt guilty about working late and, thus, having less time to spend with my family. As she could manage only evening appointments, it was only fair that *she* should take the blame for that. She began to laugh as I suggested more and more guilts that she could relieve for me, for her neighbours, her work colleagues, and others, by soaking up the blame. I also suggested to her that it would be very irresponsible of her to improve too quickly. If she were no longer to need therapy, it would deprive me of part of my income, and my children would have to go without some of their meals. She would be totally to blame for that.

CONCLUSION

Spontaneous humour, arising as it does from the unconscious, often provides access to issues and themes in therapy that have been expressed more unconsciously. Thus, therapists for whom humour is merely a distraction from the serious purpose of therapy, an irrelevance or irreverence, a denial or defense, miss out on a potentially rich source of intuitive diagnostic and therapeutic creativity. If humour is not a natural part of a therapist's repertoire, however, it is rarely therapeutic, particularly if the therapist is ambivalent about the appropriateness of its use. Self-conscious, forced, or clumsy attempts at humour can lead to embarrassment, to an interruption in the flow of an interview, and at times to a complete breakdown in rapport.

A FINAL STORY

A man came to see me for help with what he defined as a midlife crisis. Also, he was concerned that he needed to develop a greater understanding of himself, who he was, and why he found it difficult to maintain relationships. He had had a variety of therapy experiences of the exploratory/growth type and was beginning to wonder, based on these experiences, whether he had really deep-seated problems that would take time to resolve.

I introduced the notion that a belief in the presence of deep-seated problems could become, in itself, a deep-seated problem. I asked whether he would be particularly disappointed if he were to discover that all he had were a few habits that needed work, habits of response that used to be functional but were now a handicap. He seemed intrigued by this idea.

At the end of the session, he asked me whether it was important that he work to gain some insight into why he behaved the way he did. I answered that, although many therapists would disagree with me, his unconscious understood him perfectly well and that most important learnings were best left buried in the unconscious mind. The conscious mind tended to interfere and confuse things. I told him the humourous story of the centipede who, on being asked how it walked so elegantly with so many legs to control, thought about it and immediately fell over.

REFERENCES

Berger, M.M. (Ed.). (1978). *Beyond the double bind*. New York: Brunner/Mazel.

Cade, B.W. (1982). Humour and creativity. *Journal of Family Therapy, 4*, 35–42.

Cade, B.W. (1985). Unpredictability and change: A holographic metaphor. In G. Weeks (Ed.), *Promoting change through paradoxical therapy*. Homewood, IL: Dow Jones-Irwin.

de Shazer, S. (1985). *Keys to solution in brief therapy*. New York: W.W. Norton.

Erickson, M.H., & Rossi, E.L. (1976). *Hypnotic realities*. New York: Irvington.

Farrelly, F., & Brandsma, J. (1974). *Provocative therapy*. Eagle River, WI: Shields.

Fry, W.F., Jr. (1963). *Sweet madness*. Palo Alto, CA: Pacific Books.

Kane, T.R., Suls, J.M., & Tedeschi, J. (1977). Humour as a tool of interaction. In A.J. Chapman & H.C. Foot (Eds.), *It's a funny thing, humour*. Oxford: Pergamon Press.

Koestler, A. (1975). *The act of creation*. London: Picador.

Levant, R.F. (1984). *Family therapy: A comprehensive overview*. Englewood Cliffs, NJ: Prentice-Hall.

Levine, J. (1977). Humour as a form of therapy. In A.J. Chapman & H.C. Foot (Eds.), *It's a funny thing, humour*. Oxford: Pergamon Press.

Madanes, C. (1984). *Behind the one-way mirror: Advances in the practice of strategic therapy*. San Francisco: Jossey-Bass.

9

To Be Direct or Indirect . . . That is *a* Question!

Kurt Ludewig, PhD
University of Hamburg
Federal Republic of Germany
and
Director
Institute for Systems Study
Hamburg, Federal Republic of
  Germany

THE PROBLEM OF CLASSIFICATION

CLASSIFICATION HAS LONG been an indispensable tool for traditional science. So-called systemic science, however, has taken a different course; it has become the search for complementarities that bring opposing categories of thought (i.e., classifications) together. In systemic science, classifications are no longer seen as approximations of independent realities, but as reflections of the observer's cognitive structure. Unless classifications either increase the understanding of theoretical formulations or serve as a guide in practice, however, they are theoretically superfluous and/or practically irritating.

Therapeutic interventions may take many different forms, and empirical research indicates that they may all be pragmatically effective, aesthetically fitting, and ethically acceptable. If such differing approaches, ranging from giving advice and prescribing drugs, through expressing empathy, to telling stories and using hypnotic trances, may all be effective, it must be assumed that the type of intervention does not determine effectiveness. If single interventions per se were helpful, therapy could be reduced to the application of techniques, much like the repair machines.

According to Maturana (1982), the structural determinism of living systems may be "perturbed," but not purposively changed; interactions may trigger structural change, but never determine it. Change results from internally correlated compensations to a perturbation. Thus, therapeutic interventions do not work in a vacuum. On the contrary, they operate within a social context that emerges from the interactions between *this* therapist and *this* patient under *these* circumstances. Any examination of therapeutic interventions must consider the context of which they are only a part.

CASE EXAMPLE

A 55-year-old lawyer, whose condition had been diagnosed by several psychiatrists during a 20-year history of psychiatric treatment as chronic schizophrenia, engaged in therapy with two family therapists. The patient was a very intelligent person who, among other things, had used his legal knowledge to help fellow patients. Since his divorce some 10 years earlier, he had concentrated on helping young so-called schizophrenics by giving them a home in his own apartment and intense emotional support.

During the first session, he discussed his symptoms and problems with almost professional accuracy. As requested, he brought his former wife, also a lawyer, to the second session. She had remained in contact with him since the divorce and had helped him on many occasions. She reported that her ex-husband felt most satisfied when he was able to do two things: to work hard and to help the needy. At this point, the patient declared that this attitude was exactly what had made him very unhappy, because his efforts to help others had generally ended with frustration—his proteges always left him alone once they felt better.

At the end of the session, the therapists told the patient that what he had been doing—working hard and helping the needy—was exactly what a therapist does. The problem seemed to be that he had received little or no gratification for his work and, thus, he had "burned out" many times. Professional therapists, however, received a whole set of gratifications that permitted them to carry on with their difficult job: a salary, paid vacations, a team (for emotional support), and, above all, supervision. They explained that the supervision actually allows therapists to "refuel" and to eliminate much of what strains and disconcerts them. Because of this, these two therapists offered the patient occasional supervision instead of therapy in order to help the patient do his chosen work without either burning out or returning to the hospital repeatedly in order to refuel.

These therapists made no assumptions about "real health" (Ludewig, 1983). In this sense, they made no concrete efforts to "cure" the patient's "symptoms." Instead, the therapists planned to cooperate with the patient in terms of what seemed important and rewarding to him (de Shazer, 1982). Their intervention can be considered a positively connoted reframing of the therapeutic situation: the patient became a therapist; the therapists became supervisors.

Two questions require consideration: (1) Should this intervention be classified as direct or indirect? (2) How did this intervention occur to the therapists? The decision to classify this intervention as direct or indirect depends on the criteria that seem relevant to the decision maker, according to his or her own ideas about therapy. If the decision maker chooses a different criterion or a different level of consideration, however, will the classification still hold?

The second question, regarding the way in which the intervention occurred to the therapists, entails at least two levels of consideration. From the position of the therapists, the answer seems to be "Who knows?" Would the same intervention have occurred to them if the session had taken place in the morning instead of the evening? If they had done something else before beginning the session? Or, if the day had been rainy? Certainly, once they had begun asking questions about the patient's most rewarding activities, they would undoubtedly have reduced the "universe" of all possible interventions considerably. In addition, because their concept of interventions included an unexpected change in their behavior that would be a perturbation for the patient (e.g., connoting positively whatever the patient does), the range of possible interventions becomes even narrower. Does this explain the generation of this specific intervention, however? Do these initial conditions make it possible to reconstruct the steps taken to formulate it? Could it have been predicted?

From a more abstract level of theoretical assessment, the answer to the second question seems to become: "It depends!" It depends primarily on the observer's point of view. An observer may prefer to regard social interaction as an incomputable assembly of single events that defies thorough description. Or, an observer may make use of all available details to attempt a logical reconstruction and end up with a post facto explication that only appears logically coherent.

Admittedly, if a more typical intervention had been used, it might have been easier to answer both questions. The therapists might have intervened by saying, for example, "Since you are suffering from burn-out, you should stop supporting fellow patients and should pay more attention to your own needs" or "Stop relating to your former wife because that reinforces your feelings of helplessness." Would it *really* be easier to classify these interventions as direct or indirect, however? From what specific point of view?

Such considerations may appear, especially to the practitioner who seeks clarity and guidance, confusing and even annoying. Practitioners know from experience, however, that therapy is not just walking step by step up a staircase to good interventions. Like an artist, a therapist creates through therapy new worlds of experience and thus new realities. Does it matter whether the therapist's artistry resembles that of a Picasso or that of a supermarket painter?

So far, it may appear that therapeutic interventions are basically undeterminable and inaccessible to rational understanding. Yet, therapists learn considerably by observing others' work and by reading narrations of therapeutic sessions. If all that counts in personal talent (individual structure) and actual context, there would be no way to account for a therapist's education (Ludewig, 1985a).

WHAT IS THERAPY?

In general terms, therapy may be defined as an observer's description of two or more individuals who are behaving in accordance with a conjointly accepted meaning (i.e., membership or role taking within a specific process of recurrent social interaction). Unlike cells and organisms, a social group—a structured aggregation of individuals—shows no topological border; therefore, it can be distinguished by an observer only in the domain of consensual meaning (semantics).

In defining the therapeutic system, the distinction between organization and structure of a system proposed by Maturana (1982) is applicable. Organization is defined by the relationships between components that must exist before a system can be identified as a member of a class of systems; structure, by the relationships between the concrete components that constitute a particular system under observation. The organization of a small face-to-face social system, such as a group or a family, consists of the expected relationships between the involved roles, whereas its structure is constituted by the actual role takers. That means that, in order to identify a group as of a specific kind, it is necessary to be aware of the constituting roles and the conditions under which they may be distinguished. Furthermore, in order to describe a particular group, the observer must decide whether the observed individuals are performing the corresponding roles.

The distinction between organization and structure makes it clear that many different structures may embody a particular kind of social system; therapies and families are obvious examples of this diversity. In the case of therapy, its definition entails three conditions of distinguishability:

1. At least one of the members must take and retain throughout the duration of therapy the therapist's role.

2. At least one other member must take and retain the complementary patient's role.

3. In order to distinguish this configuration from related ones, such as welfare, friendship, or control, the relationship between the roles must entail time-limitation.

If any of these conditions is not fulfilled, the observer cannot identify the observed system as a therapeutic one.

WHAT IS THE THERAPIST'S ROLE?

Clearly, there could be no therapy and no patient without a therapist. The patient's role, being a complement of the therapist's role, requires no further specification than the actual role taker's acceptance of the therapist as such. Thus, the therapist's role is more crucial, and the observer must have criteria that make it possible to discern which observed behaviors are those of the therapist, which should be ascribed to the personal style of the actual performer, and which are altogether strange to therapy.

According to biological epistemology, change in living systems is always determined by the structure of the system, that is, by the internal relationships that occur to compensate for perturbations; change is not determined by the perturbation itself or by the perturbing agent. This implies that therapeutic interventions may only trigger change (compensation). Therapists, then, face a dilemma; they must trigger change without ever knowing precisely how they should do it or what the results will be. In this sense, the therapist's role cannot be defined in terms of the effects of therapeutic behavior, but must be defined in terms of intercorrelated behavior patterns. This being the case, a theoretically coherent definition of the therapist's role may be derived only from an explicit theory of human relationships and of therapy.

Therapists have coped with this dilemma in many different ways. Their solutions may be ordered along a continuum that ranges from "be yourself" to "follow the instructions." Epistemologically, the extreme solutions reflect the perspective assumed by the observer/ theoretician. The observer who views the therapist as someone who is inside the interactional network will realize that the therapist is being himself or herself. From this perspective, the only recommendation that may be given to the therapist is to act at every moment as the best possible "self" by enriching his or her personal experience.

On the other hand, the observer who focuses on the therapist as someone who is acting on a system from the outside will regard the relationship between therapist and patient as a one-sided source of input. Consequently, the recommendation given to the therapist is to follow the proper instructions for the case at stake. If this recommendation is generalized, however, therapy may no longer be considered the process of a system composed of human beings. Ethics is bound to give way to pragmatics. Even so, it may at times prove useful to regard therapy as a relationship of heteronomous systems, because this abstraction may enable the therapist to plan interventions *as if* they were determining inputs or instructions for the patient system.

A comprehensive solution to the therapist's dilemma should be "Do both!" Therapists have attained a high degree of flexibility when they behave alternately as someone inside the therapeutic system and as someone outside the system. In this way, therapists can both share experiences with the patient(s) and plan interventions. Such an integration of therapeutic approaches provides therapists with a clear orientation to guide their behavior during therapy and allows for personal adaptations as required by the circumstances of a particular therapy.

Ludewig (1985b) attempted such an integration in formulating rules or recommendations to outline the therapist's role. His rules included:

- Define yourself as a therapist.
- Connote yourself positively.
- Ask constructive questions.
- Intervene sparingly.
- Be modest.
- Be brief.

Provided that such guidelines are not understood as ready-to-reproduce recipes, they constrict the personal possibilities of a therapist only as much as required to conserve identity and adaptation as a therapist throughout the process of therapy.

DIRECTNESS VS. INDIRECTNESS: A SIGNIFICANT DISTINCTION?

In order to determine whether it is useful for theory and practice to distinguish between direct and indirect therapeutic techniques, it is necessary to ask the following questions:

1. Does this polarization help the observer discern whether what is being observed may be considered therapy?

2. Does it help the practitioner conserve his or her role identity and adaptation as a therapist?

The answer to the first question must be "It depends!" It depends on the unit that the observer has chosen for observation. If the observer focuses on content, an intervention that does not explicitly address a given problem could be classified as indirect. If the observer prefers to focus on behavioral patterns, an intervention that does not address a concrete problem may well directly address some relevant pattern of the patient or the therapeutic system, as demonstrated by de Shazer and Molnar (1984). If, on the other hand, the observer bases distinctions on the therapist's intentions, an intervention may be considered direct if it is designed to change the patient and indirect if it is designed to promote joining. Thus, the distinction between direct and indirect therapy does not provide the observer with reliable criteria for the identification of therapy; with regard to the formulation of the theory of therapy, it is superfluous.

As to the question of the practical usefulness of this classification, the answer must be once again: "It depends!" It depends on the definitions of therapy and the therapist's role. If therapy is regarded as the process of creating a structure between autonomous individuals, the actual manifestation of this process is determined by the position of the participants within the social system that they build. Actual interventions

emerge as the result of interplay between the participants in the given roles. At this level of consideration, the distinction between directness and indirectness proves irrelevant for practice.

If, from a more concrete standpoint, the therapist is supposed to adapt to the patient system (i.e., cooperate [de Shazer, 1982]), while simultaneously eliciting unexpected behaviors that are likely to trigger compensatory change in patients, the distinction between direct and indirect interventions may be of some pragmatic utility. Viewing intervention from different sides may help therapists with a given personal style and theory of therapy to enrich their repertoire of possible interventions. Yet, taking into consideration the fact that therapists must always act on the spot, based on events that occur during the session, compliance with a previously standardized program (e.g., "intervene indirectly whenever . . .") may be more troublesome than useful. Such compliance may not only reduce the therapist's adaptive flexibility, but also promote the discomfort and so-called resistance in a patient who feels like an object of techniques instead of a subject of interaction. In that case, therapy would have ceased being therapy and become a system of another kind (e.g., control or struggle).

In sum, the classification of interventions depends on the observer. Such dissimilar interventions as setting behavioral rules and telling farfetched stories may be considered both direct and indirect. Erickson's well-known stories (Haley, 1973) may serve as an example of directness, since it is said that he always kept his interventions very close to what he considered to be the patient's problem. (Probably even he would not have been able to decide whether his interventions were direct or indirect!) Alternatively, the intervention of a consulting school psychologist who advises a mother on ways to treat her child could be considered indirect, since the psychologist is proposing that a family member do things that will, to some extent, affect many others.

As long as no assumptions are made concerning the "real" nature of interventions, the question of directness or indirectness in therapy reveals itself as a matter of personal style. This would be a trivial assertion if it did not refer to a social interaction that implies as much human responsibility as therapy does.

REFERENCES

de Shazer, S. (1982). *Patterns of brief family therapy*. New York: Guilford Press.

de Shazer, S., & Molnar, A. (1984). Changing teams/changing families. *Family Process, 23,* 481–486.

Haley, J. (1973). *Uncommon therapy: The psychiatric techniques of Milton H. Erickson.* New York: Norton.

Ludewig, K. (1983). Die Therapeutische Intervention. In K. Schneider (Ed.), *Familientherapie.* Paderborn: Junfermann.

Ludewig, K. (1985a). Aspects, problems, solutions, scruples concerning systemic therapy teaching. *Zeitschrift fur systemische therapie, 3,* 132–140.

Ludewig, K. (1985b). Ten commandments (plus one): A brief outline for a systemic theory of therapy, practice, and evaluation. Unpublished manuscript.

Maturana, H. (1982). *Erkennen: Die organisation und verkoerperung von wirklichkeit* (Reader). Braunschweig: Vieweg.

Index

Czechoslovak Medical Society J.E. Purkyně
is pleased to announce the

INTERNATIONAL CONGRESS ON FAMILY THERAPY

"The Patterns Which Connect"
to be held in

PRAGUE, CZECHOSLOVAKIA on MAY 11-15, 1987

featuring

MAURIZIO ANDOLFI, EDGAR AUERSWALD, MARY CATHERINE BATESON, DONALD BLOCH, LUIGI BOSCOLO, GIANFRANCO CECCHIN, JOSEF DUSS-VON WERDT, MONY ELKAIM, KITTY LA PERRIERE, SALVADOR MINUCHIN, DAVID REISS, VIRGINIA SATIR, MARA SELVINI-PALAZZOLI, CARLOS SLUZKI, HELM STIERLIN, GEORGE VASSILIOU, JÜRG WILLI, LYMAN WYNNE, JEFFREY ZEIG and other distinguished presenters.

For further information please contact:
Czechoslovak Medical Society—ICFT 1987
Vít. února 31, P.O. Box 88
120 26 Praha 2, Czechoslovakia

Petr Boš, M.D.
Secretary General